T0254843

Lecture Notes in Computer Science 13279

Agnieszka Gryszczyńska · Przemysław Polański ·
Nils Gruschka · Kai Rannenberg ·
Monika Adamczyk (Eds.)

Privacy Technologies and Policy

10th Annual Privacy Forum, APF 2022
Warsaw, Poland, June 23–24, 2022
Proceedings

Editors
Agnieszka Gryszczyńska ⓘ
Cardinal Stefan Wyszyński University
in Warsaw
Warsaw, Poland

Nils Gruschka ⓘ
University of Oslo
Oslo, Norway

Monika Adamczyk ⓘ
ENISA
Athens, Greece

Przemysław Polański
Koźmiński University
Warsaw, Poland

Kai Rannenberg
Goethe University Frankfurt
Frankfurt, Germany

ISSN 0302-9743   ISSN 1611-3349 (electronic)
Lecture Notes in Computer Science
ISBN 978-3-031-07314-4   ISBN 978-3-031-07315-1 (eBook)
https://doi.org/10.1007/978-3-031-07315-1

This Springer imprint is published by the registered company Springer Nature Switzerland AG
The registered company address is: Gewerbestrasse 11, 6330 Cham, Switzerland

Preface

With this volume we introduce the proceedings of the 2022 edition of the Annual Privacy Forum (APF). APF 2022 was co-organized by the European Union Agency for Cybersecurity (ENISA), DG Connect of the European Commission, the Cardinal Stefan Wyszyński University in Warsaw, and Koźmiński University. The conference was hosted in Warsaw, Poland. This conference, already in its 10th edition, was established as an opportunity to bring together key communities, namely policy, academia, and industry, in the broader area of privacy and data protection while focusing on privacy-related application areas.

Like in the previous edition, a large focus of the 2022 conference was on the General Data Protection Regulation (GDPR).

There were 38 submissions in response to the APF call for papers. Each paper was peer-reviewed by three members of the international Program Committee (PC). On the basis of significance, novelty, and scientific quality, eight papers were selected (a 21% acceptance rate) and are compiled in this volume. The papers are organized across four thematic areas:

- Users' Rights ("A Generic Data Model for Implementing Right of Access Requests", "Can Authoritative Governments Abuse the Right to Access?");
- Security of Personal Data ("The Data Protection Implications of the EU AML Framework: A Critical Overview & the Case of AI", "Data Protection and Machine-Learning-Supported Decision-Making at the EU Border: ETIAS Profiling Under Scrutiny");
- Privacy Enhancing Technologies ("Application-oriented Selection of Privacy Enhancing Technologies", "Fifty Shades of Personal Data – Partial Re-identification and GDPR");
- Privacy Engineering ("Google and Apple Exposure Notifications System: Exposure Notifications or Notified Exposures?", "Analysis and Constructive Criticism of the Official Data Protection Impact Assessment of the German Corona-Warn-App").

We wish to thank the members of the PC, for devoting their time to reviewing the submitted papers and providing constructive feedback, the authors, whose papers make up the bulk of the content of this conference, and the attendees, whose interest in the conference is the main driver for its organization.

June 2022

Agnieszka Gryszczyńska
Przemysław Polański
Nils Gruschka
Kai Rannenberg
Monika Adamczyk

Organization

General Co-chairs

Agnieszka Gryszczyńska	Cardinal Stefan Wyszyński University in Warsaw, Poland
Przemysław Polanski	Koźmiński University, Poland
Nils Gruschka	University of Oslo, Norway
Kai Rannenberg	Goethe University Frankfurt, Germany
Monika Adamczyk	ENISA, Greece

Program Committee

Harsha Banavara	S&C Electric, USA
Bettina Berendt	Katholieke Universiteit Leuven, Belgium
Athena Bourka	ENISA, Greece
Jerzy Cytowski	Cardinal Stefan Wyszyński University in Warsaw, Poland
Kamil Czaplicki	Cardinal Stefan Wyszyński University in Warsaw, Poland
Giuseppe D'Acquisto	Garante per la protezione dei dati personali, Italy
José M. Del Álamo	Universidad Politécnica de Madrid, Spain
Matteo Dell'Amico	EURECOM, France
Diana Dimitrova	FIZ Karlsruhe, Germany
Piotr Drobek	Cardinal Stefan Wyszyński University in Warsaw, Poland
Prokopios Drogkaris	ENISA, Greece
Petros Efstathopoulos	Symantec Research Labs, USA
Anna Fabijańska	Technical University of Łódź, Poland
Paweł Fajgielski	John Paul II Catholic University of Lublin, Poland
Ana Ferreira	University of Porto, Portugal
Simone Fischer-Hübner	Karlstad University, Sweden
Michael Friedewald	Fraunhofer ISI, Germany
Marta Fydrych-Gąsowska	mBank S.A., Poland
Agnieszka Grzelak	Koźmiński University, Poland
Jassim Happa	Royal Holloway, University of London, UK
Szymon Jaroszewicz	Polish Academy of Sciences, Poland

Organizers

Contents

Users' Rights

A Generic Data Model for Implementing Right of Access Requests

Malte Hansen[1,2(✉)] and Meiko Jensen[3(✉)]

[1] Kiel University of Applied Sciences, Kiel, Germany
Malte.Hansen@fh-kiel.de
[2] University of Oslo, Oslo, Norway
[3] Karlstad University, Karlstad, Sweden
Meiko.Jensen@kau.se

Abstract. According to Article 15 of the GDPR, data subjects have the right to access personal data handled by data controllers and their processors. This raises demand for a dedicated technical service implementation in order to create valid, complete, and legally compliant responses to such requests.

In this paper, we provide both a Data Request Model and a Response Data Model for answering such requests on a technical level. While outlining the overall process of handling such a request, we showcase a set of requirements that needs to be fulfilled, and we discuss a set of issues commonly arising in such an Article 15 service implementation.

Keywords: Article 15 · GDPR · Right of Access · Data Request Model · Response Data Model

1 Introduction

A key element in the current European data strategy (cf. [18]) is the proliferation of a pan-European data market, with personal data of citizens being provided to data consumers, such as research organizations or companies, on demand. For instance, the European Data Governance Act (cf. [37]) defines the role of *data intermediaries* that store and process personal data on behalf of the data subjects, and manage access requests by third-party organizations to such data. Here, the data intermediaries have to fulfil a set of obligations, such as a strict prohibition of utilizing the data for any other purposes than those defined in the law. Especially, a data intermediary is required to maintain and cater for all data subject rights according to the European General Data Protection Regulation (GDPR Art 15 ff., [40]).

In light of this ongoing development, the challenge of managing data subject rights in a reasonable technical manner becomes evident. For instance, answers to a request according to Art. 15 GDPR ("Right of Access") must be provided

---

The contribution of M. Jensen was partly funded by the Swedish Foundation for Strategic Research (SSF SURPRISE) project.

A. Gryszczyńska et al. (Eds.): APF 2022, LNCS 13279, pp. 3–22, 2022.
https://doi.org/10.1007/978-3-031-07315-1_1

to the requester in a timely manner, free of charge, and "in a commonly used electronic form" [40, Art. 15 (3)3]. Especially for larger organizations, this is only feasible if a dedicated technical infrastructure for catering for such Right of Access requests is implemented.

In this paper, we analyze the specific requirements for such a technical infrastructure for answering Right of Access requests. We focus on the most challenging aspects, such as request initiation, data subject authentication, data models for request and response, and the overall process of a Right of Access request.

The paper is organized as follows. First, we discuss the state of the art in implementing Article 15 requests. Then, Sect. 2 provides legal and technical requirements for the proposed models and process. The specific aspects of the Data Request Model are discussed in Sect. 3, followed by the Response Data Model in Sect. 4. The overall process is subsumed and evaluated in Sect. 5, and the paper concludes with future research directions in Sect. 6.

1.1 The GDPR and Article 15

The General Data Protection Regulation [40] is a regulation that aims towards increasing the control citizens of the European Union (EU) and European Economic Area have about their personal data, promoting privacy by design and creating a shared legislative foundation for data protection and privacy inside the EU.

The terminology for the different actors used in the GDPR, which will also be used in this work, can be derived from Article 4 as follows:

- Data Subject (DS), addressing the individuals behind the personal data
- Data Controller (DC), depicting the entities responsible for the data collection
- Data Processor (DP), describing the entities that collect, process and/or forward the data on behalf of the DC

In order to improve readability, the term DC is used to address both DCs and DPs in the remainder of this paper, as the right of access extends to all DPs of a DC – despite legal responsibility remaining solely with the DC.

GDPR Articles 5 and 6 define the lawfulness of processing. Processing of personal data is only lawful in case of at least one of the following conditions:

- The DS has explicitly given consent
- Fulfillment of contractual obligations
- Compliance with legal obligations of a DC
- Protection of vital interests of the DS or another natural person
- Performance of tasks of public interest or execution of official authority
- Fulfillment of legitimate interests of the DC or a third party, where fundamental rights and freedoms of the DS are not breached

Especially, Article 5 introduces the data minimization principle. Data minimization restricts the collection of personal data to information which is adequate, relevant and necessary for the purposes of the processing.

Further, various rights are granted to the DS by the GDPR. Some prominent ones include:

- The DC must relay information to the DS in a transparent and easily comprehensible way (Art. 12)
- Right of rectification, giving the DS the right to have inaccurate data be corrected (Art. 16)
- Right to erasure, allowing the DS to request deletion of all personal data related itself (Art. 17)
- Right to restriction of processing (Art. 18) or right to object processing for marketing purposes or processing not necessary for the provided service (Art. 21)
- Right to data portability, allowing the DS to request a full copy of his complete personal data from a DC for itself or another DC in a timely manner (Art. 20)

One essential DS right given by the GDPR is the Right of Access by the data subject, codified in Article 15. Article 15 grants the DS the right to know if their personal data is being processed by a DC and the right to access processed data and receive the information about it. The scope of this information will be laid out in Sect. 2. A copy of this information can be requested from the DC by the DS, as long as the rights and freedoms of others are not breached. Requests made online have to be answered in a commonly used electronic form.

To advance the development of a data model for interoperability, Pandit et al. [31] have devised the information flows between the different entities, involved in GDPR processes. An adopted version of this work can be seen in Fig. 1. Two further entities of relevance here are the Data Protection Authorities (DPA) and Seals & Certifications. The former are public institutions that handle complaints about DCs by DSs and monitor the compliance of DCs and DPs with the GDPR. The latter are a tool, embedded in the GDPR itself, for DCs and DPs to certificate GDPR compliance for a time period of maximum three years.

1.2 State of the Art

Before taking a look at the current state of the art in context of GDPR compliance and the overall quality of requests in accordance with Article 15, it is important to note, that the GDPR itself does not specify how to implement its articles. The Article 29 Working Party has released guidelines on how to adapt some aspects of the GDPR, however, these do not cover the whole scope of the regulation. Since then, the Article 29 Working Party has been replaced by the European Data Protection Board (EDPB), which has endorsed all of the previously released guidelines concerning the GDPR [17].

The GDPR, compliance with it and potential shortcomings or lack of specification are matters that have been discussed frequently since its introduction. Ogriseg discusses the lack of protection of employees' personal data [30]. The right to data portability faces several technical challenges [7] and its lack of

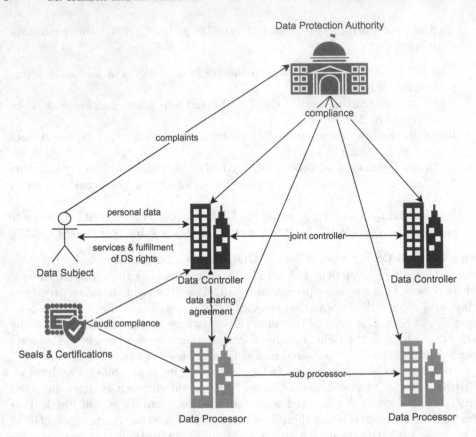

Fig. 1. Information flows between different entities in the context of the GDPR, according to [31]

unambiguity may lead to a multitude of different results in practice (e.g. [14,16]). Enforcement of DS rights granted by the GDPR proves to be difficult in non-EU based entities [22]. As Article 15 was one of the articles that counted the most fined violations in the first year of the GDPR (see [4]), this is a major challenge to face. First approaches to tackle cross-border data transfers do, however, exist [23].

When asking Norwegian companies about the biggest challenges concerning the GDPR, Presthus et al. [36] found that 46% of participants have a limited understanding of the GDPR, 23% lack budget and 18% lack the technology required to comply with the new regulation. Additionally 21% reported Article 15 as one of the articles of greatest concern. As the technology, budget and IT environment of every company is unique, solutions for GDPR compliance are hard to generalize and hence a variety of approaches exist. To tackle these challenges, research has started for static analysis [19], small- and medium-sized enterprises [10], the linkage of purpose and business processes [5] and privacy engineering [29]. Huth [26] has released a pattern catalog for GDPR compliant data protection, which proposes several research questions, which will be covered in the next section.

On the consumer side, according to a survey by Quermann and Degeling [38], 93% of EU citizens surveyed stated that they think mobile applications share their data without their consent. One year after implementation of the GDPR, Presthus and Sørum [35] found that, while being better informed about their rights, consumers don't execute their rights. Additionally, almost 40% of the participants thought they have no control over their personal data, with lack of trust in the DCs being a main concern.

To gauge the current level of compliance with Article 15, as well as the quality of the responses, a look into existing research on Article 15 requests is necessary. Apart from pre-GDPR previous work [25], Bufalieri et al. [11], Alizadeh et al. [1], and Presthus and Sørum [35] conducted investigations into Article 15 requests and found that, while most companies respond to the request in time, the information given in the given data is not sufficient. This is especially severe when the purpose and automated decision-making are concerned. Another problem that needs to be addressed is the misuse of the right to access to steal personal data. Cagnazzo et al. [12] used slighty modified email-addresses to falsely receive another DS's, partly sensitive, personal data from 10 out of 14 tested companies. A different approach by Di Martino et al. [15], using Impersonation techniques with the help of social engineering, resulted in 15 out of 55 cases of leaked data. These findings are backed by Pavur and Knerr [32], who, also, used social engineering attacks to receive personal data roughly 25% of the approached entities that sent an response. Further, 15% of the other entities required an additional form of authentication that they believed to be easily be bypassed.

1.3 Goals

Taking the state of the art into consideration, the biggest problems with the Right of Access are

- (1) the lack of know-how and technologies to implement appropriate measures to fulfill the request,
- (2) insufficient comprehensibility for the DS, especially when the purpose of data processing is concerned,
- (3) the abuse of the article to steal personal data, mostly utilizing social engineering, and
- (4) the lack of standardization and interoperability between the information systems of the different entities.

To consistently provide usable DR results, a model for the fulfillment of DRs in accordance with Article 15 of the GDPR is necessary. This model shall provide compliance with GDPR requirements, promote Privacy by Design, and consider different, common technologies, used in the information systems of DCs.

The process of the Right of Access request needs to be improved as well. A successful implementation of the model should lead to the following improvements for DRs:

- Security against applicable web security attacks
- Increased accessibility of the DR for the DS
- Increased quality and completeness of the DR answer
- Increased comprehensibility of the DR answer for the DS
- Easy processibility of the DR answer by tools, such as databases, scripting and analysis tools
- Automation of DR process
- Shorter response time
- Fewer resources needed by DC to implement satisfactory solution for DRs

It is important to note that these goals are not measurable without organizations implementing the proposed model. This is important to keep in mind during the evaluation of the model.

While the Right of Access does apply for both physical and electronic records of personal data, we will assume that the DC implemented or plans to implement an adequate data model, as a physical process directly contradicts the goals of automation and shorter response time.

2 Requirements

The purpose of the DR-model is to produce a consistent, complete and secure response for a DR according to Article 15 of the GDPR. Therefore, we must take a look at Article 15 itself and observe what it requires of the DCs to include in their answers to the DRs:

- Purpose of the processing of personal data
- Categories of personal data concerned
- Recipients or categories of recipients of the data
- Time frame of the storage of data and how this time frame is determined
- Source of the data if not collected from the DS
- Existence of automated decision-making, including meaningful information about involved logic, and significance and consequences for the DS
- Safeguards in case of transfer of data to a non-EU entity
- Copy of this data in a commonly used electronic form
- This copy must not interfere with the rights and freedoms of others

Inside these requirements some further definitions need to be made. Firstly, what exactly are the categories of personal data? In addition to the definition of personal data, as described in Sect. 1.1, Article 4 (13)(14)(15) states three special categories of personal data: genetic data, biometric data, and health data. Article 9 restricts the processing of these special categories. It further expands the special categories of personal data by information regarding:

- Racial or ethnic origin
- Political opinions
- Religious or philosophical beliefs
- Trade union membership
- Sex life or sexual orientation

While not directly described as a category, Recital 30 of the GDPR expands on online identifiers, originating from technical sources, that are utilized for profiling and identification. For the purpose of this work, this also functions as its own category.

The second thing that needs to be specified is the phrase *meaningful information* in the context of automated decision-making. The main problem is to provide information about the involved logic. Interface-based approaches to deliver explanations and transparency to the user struggle as they would reveal information about the system that the DCs do not want to disclose [34]. Approaches to circumvent this problem by not revealing knowledge about the algorithm with counterfactuals exist (cf. e.g. [43]). However, further research is required to make this a feasible option for widespread usage. As a result, meaningful information about the logic involved can only be provided consistently to a degree to which the DC can keep its underlying algorithm protected. The significance and consequences for the DS can, on the other side, be explained better, as this can be achieved by stating the purposes and further use cases of the results of the automated decision-making.

Concerning the answer of the DC, the copy of the data must be in a commonly used electronic form. While the GDPR does not define the term commonly used electronic form, Article 20, the right to data portability, requires the data in a structured, commonly used and machine-readable format. As the DCs need to comply with the other articles, besides Article 15, anyways, we can upgrade the term with these keywords. This also allows us to meet our goal of easy processibility of the DR result. But not every DS has the ability to interpret machine-readable data formats. To not forgo the goal of increased comprehensibility for the DS, an alternative for people without technical knowledge is needed as well.

3 Data Request Model

The model for data requests per Article 15 of the GDPR requires three components:

- (1) An easily locatable and operable *initiation interface* to let the DS start the DR process;
- (2) An *authentication system to indubitably confirm the identity of the DS;*
- (3) A *DR Response Building System* based on a data model that can provide the personal data of the DS completely and automatically, while complying with the requirements of the Right of Access.

3.1   Initiation Interface

The job of the initiation interface is to provide the DS with the opportunity to express their desire to enforce the Right of Access to sending the DC the respective parameters. In a minimalistic solution, the only parameter strictly required is the claimed identity of the DS, as the interface implicitly expresses the formal request for the enforcement of Article 15. This means, the DS must not enter any additional information besides their identity. Exceptions to this can be made in case the system includes additional functionalities, such as enforcement of other DS rights, or specifying limitations to the data requested, e.g. by declaring a time period, purpose or source.

Generally speaking, the initiation interface should be placed on the website or similar standard interaction surface of the applications or services concerned. If an application with a graphical user interface exists, e.g. as a mobile app, the interface should be reachable directly over the navigation menu or through the privacy tab of that application. For user accounts with privacy and data tabs, these options are viable alternatives.

Alternatively, the initiation of interaction could be offered through a dedicated API. While not offering high usability for DSs, especially ones without technology affinity, an API would allow the usage of specialized tools and software for GDPR DRs. This can lead to full automation of the DR, as the process can theoretically be completed without any input by the DS.

3.2   Authentication

In Sect. 1.2, vulnerabilities to authentication attacks, especially social engineering attacks, were discussed. To combat these deficiencies, an authentication process that is robust against common and known authentication attacks is needed. While the state of the art offers a wide variety of authentication methods for Right of Access requests, such as multi-factor authentication (MFA, [42]) or pseudonym-based authentication (e.g. the data subject authenticating itself by revealing a secret pseudonym utilized in every interaction with the DC), the success of each solution depends on the environment it is applied to. For this purpose, we discuss three different scenarios for DCs holding a different amount of information about the DS.

Scenario 1: No User Account or Email The DC holds no data of the DS besides the personal data gathered for the processing in consideration. No information with the purpose of authenticating the DS exists in the system of the DC. As the DC has not established a method of authentication with the DS and the DC should not gather additional information explicitly for authenticating a DS, the options for this scenario are the most limited.

The first possibility is to use the existing information about the DS to establish a shared secret between the two parties. The best basis for this shared secret would be exclusive and unique information that is not accessible for third parties. Usable options would be a customer, membership or specific order number.

This approach does have its flaws, though. A first hurdle is, that the DS might not have access to the information, chosen as the secret. They could've lost the documents containing the order number. Additionally, the DC has to take measures so an attacker can not guess the secret, e.g. by estimating a incrementally increasing customer number. Consequently, the shared secret should be a randomly generated information, known to both parties. To avoid replay attacks and shoulder surfing, the secret should not be reused for a later authentication request, just like an one-time password (OTP).

Using OTP technologies to deliver an authentication token to the DS is challenging in this scenario. The DC requires an communication channel that lets them securely deliver the token to the DS. Email is not a viable channel in this case, as the DC does not hold an email address of the DS and it is usually not feasible for the DC to unambiguously link a newly entered email address to the DS. If the DC has the mobile phone number of the DS, it can be used to deliver the token, for example via text messaging. Otherwise it faces the same problem email does. The home address could be used to physically send tokens as well. However, using postal services is incredibly slow and would clash with the stated goals for automation and improved processing time.

When considering the usage of identity providers (IP), we face similar problems as we did with OTPs. How can the DC assert, without having a confirmed email address or linked account, that the identity provided by the IP is that of the DS? Additionally, the usage of an IP would include a third party in the process. For an IP to be a viable authentication solution in this scenario, it must securely, reliably, and unambiguously identify and authenticate the DS as the natural person. An external confirmation of the security and trustworthiness of the IP, like a certificate issued by an official organization, could aid DCs in finding legitimate IPs.

Scenario 2: Only Email. The DC has an email address that was confirmed by the DS. As some authentication methods could not reliably be used without an email address during Scenario 1, the number of viable options for the DC increases.

Looking at challenge-response methods, the DC can implement a shared secret in the same way they can in Scenario 1. The additional information available does not help in generating a secure, exclusive secret, as an email address can often be widely known or public knowledge and is most likely used in different contexts as well.

The email address adds a reliable way to deploy OTP tokens to the DS. However, as most DS will most likely employ their email address over a third party, the DC has to be careful following this approach. Using End-to-end encryption protocols provides a secure way to utilize OTPs over email. While the common email protocols are equipped to assert confidentiality, authenticity, and integrity, not all email providers support the use of these protocols [20]. Thus, the DC has to ensure that proper protocols for secure email communication are usable with the email provider, before accepting this authentication method. Viable end-to-end protocols for email services include S/MIME [39] and OpenPGP [13].

Using an IP is also easier in this scenario, as the email address can serve as the bridge between the DC and IP. While this does increase the number of IPs that can provide authentication of the DS to the DC, it does not eliminate the other problems, described in the previous section.

Scenario 3: User Account with Email. The DC has a user account that is directly linked to the DS. The account does not necessarily have to contain the DS's real name, but can use some other identifier, such as a customer ID, to link the data to the account. Part of this information is an email address, confirmed by the DS. The DS can log into their account by entering the username or email address in combination with a password, that was previously selected by the DS.

The existence of a password protected user account is an easily implementable authentication method, to use for DRs as well. Static passwords are not very secure in comparison with other authentication methods, though [9,27]. Encryption and adequate complexity requirements are necessary to reach an acceptable security threshold. To circumvent attacks from unsupervised computers, the DS must also not be omitted from reentering the password in case they are already logged in. Additionally the authentication database must be secured appropriately. For example, Blue and Furey have introduced an approach to get authentication databases up to date with GDPR guidelines [6].

The other authentication methods can be employed as in the previous scenario.

Special Scenarios. While implementing RFID is challenging due to the hardware required, a DC may have already established a working RFID authentication and deployed RFID tags and readers to their users. E.g., a bank might use a combination of RFID tag on a bank card and TAN-generator to let customers legitimize their transactions or other services. As the security offered by a properly implemented RFID solution is very high, usability is great, and implementation is mostly already in place, existent RFID solutions are a strongly recommended option for an authentication factor.

Biometrics are offering high security. However, they are highly sensitive personal data and should not be collected and saved by a DC unless they are indispensable for carrying out their service. However, some systems may have already implemented biometric based authentication schemes, such as using fingerprints in mobile apps to authenticate the owner of the phone. Importantly, this example would allow for the fingerprints to be saved locally on the DS's phone. Even though this scenario would lead to biometric based authentication without the need to store or transmit the biometrics itself, some questions need to be answered before accepting such an authentication scheme for DRs: Can the scheme consistently be implemented on the DS's devices? Can it be easily operated by the DS? How secure is the scheme? How can the DC assert no tampering takes place without access to the device?

4   Response Data Model

4.1   Article 20 Related Challenges

Adopting a data model for compliance with Article 15 of the GDPR is fruitless, if it creates conflicts with other DS rights. Article 20 shares similarities with Article 15 and allows us to further define some aspects of Article 15 that have room for interpretation, such as the data format.

Recital 63 of the GDPR states that the purpose of the right to data portability is to allow secure exchange of data between DCs, while strengthening the control rights of the DS on their data. The realization of Article 20 does come with technical challenges, presented by Bozdag [7], that impact Article 15 and the architecture of this data model as well:

Raw vs Inferred Data. DCs are obligated to make raw data portable, while the same does not apply for inferred data. The challenge is identifying a data set as raw or inferred, as the same information can be raw or inferred data, depending on how it was generated. For Article 15 the nature of the data set does not matter, as long as it is being processed. However, adding the nature of the information to the data model, e.g. by clarifying its source, allows the DS to better monitor compliance with Article 20.

Tagging for Legal Ground. Article 20 only covers data collected under consent or contract. This means, that a field for the legal ground is required for our data model. Problematic is the handling of existing data sets, as these do not necessarily contain this information. Not tagging these data sets may lead to personal data being wrongfully omitted from the enforcement of Article 20. Applying false tags to data and making it portable would violate data minimization.

How to Determine 3rd Party Affection. Executing Article 20 or 15 is not possible for a DS if the enforcement affects the rights and freedoms of others. This means, that data sets containing information about third parties need special consideration. While a data protection officer (DPO) can investigate the data set during a manual processing of the DRs, this is not possible for an automated process. To solve this issue, the data model must contain a field to clarify the status of data sets containing personal data from more than one DS. Declaring the correct status is another challenge, as the status depends on the context. Therefore it is difficult to develop a general algorithm for this purpose. This means that solutions covering various scenarios or individual solutions by the DC are necessary to aid the data model in determining the affection of third parties.

Article 11 and Exemption from Portability. If the DC can not clearly identify the DS in the data set, they must not obligate with the portability request. This applies to the right of access as well. Prove of identity provided by the DS does allow the DS to exert their rights as normal. But, DCs with anonymized data sets might not have the expertise required to use the proof of identification, delivered by the DS, to re-identify the data set. For the data model this means that it must be able to group different identifiers together to build a complete data set belonging to a DS. Individual data sets have to be independent though, as a prove of identification is still required.

Format. As covered in Sect. 2, the required format of the copy of data is a commonly used, machine readable, structured format. Which formats fulfill these requirements depend on the context. To have the DS not rely on any specific program to process the copy, the format should be selected from the current solutions that are accepted and workable by most current data base systems. The copy can then be taken from the data base by the process, before being transformed into the desired format. Current formats include JSON [8] and CSV [41]. The problem is, that these formats are not easily readable for DS without technical know-how. Hence, another format, focused on comprehensibility by humans, is needed.

When discussing the implementation of the right for data portability, De Hert et al. introduce two different approaches: A restrictive approach, and the recommended extensive approach [14]. The restrictive approach deletes the data from the originating DC, while the extensive approach aims to fuse the data sets, creating a more complete data set, allowing for more interoperability between services. Considering the data model, both approaches might lead to the DS losing overview about the source and purpose of collection of their data. Either because the origin was deleted, possibly deleting the record of the legal ground for this information, or because it is not clear which source contributed which information to the fused data set. This strengthens the need for a clear tagging of the source of the data, which must be kept during the processing, transfer and fusion of data.

4.2 Exploring a Traceable Data Trail

For the DS to be able to comprehend which DCs and DPs hold their data at which time, for which purpose, they require a data trail they are able to follow.

To create a usable data trail, we need to be able to attach information to data, that is kept, while it is transferred between different entities. One approach to achieve this are sticky policies [33]. Sticky policies are machine-readable policies that are attached to data. The content of the policies depend on the implementation. Use cases include proposed usage, allowed platforms and frameworks, obligations, specification of the time frame, and lists of trusted authorities. For our purpose the processing purposes, sources and destinations, and the legal ground are thinkable, additional attachments. Having sticky policies, that are embedded in the underlying system, allows for GDPR compliant automated decision-making and facilitates monitoring and auditing the data. On the downside, sticky policies come with a data overhead.

A solution to create a controllable data trail, compliant with Privacy-by-Design and the GDPR, is the framework privacyTracker [21]. PrivacyTracker consists of four components:

Customer Record the data structure consisting of Record Identification in the form of an URI, user email address, initial and local creation time and expiration time, Data Traceability in the form of forward, backward, and backward-to-root references, and Cryptographic Controls for the original record and signature.

Collection Module an interface for customizable registration applications.

Distribution Module managing the distribution of customer data to a requesting party over the API.

Traceability Module constructing the data trail for the Customer Record, recovering the data set from unavailable link references and implementing the right to erasure.

Based on this information, advanced data track tools like visualizations can be applied (cf. e.g. [2,28]), as well as other tools assisting the DS in managing their specific privacy preferences and requirements.

4.3   Required Classes

Considering the legal requirements and two previous paragraphs means that a satisfactory data model has to include a data set class, containing adequate attributes, fulfilling the legal requirements and allowing to build a complete data trail. Additionally, the data set class has to be catered by classes for DSs, DPs, categories of personal data, and processing purposes, as seen in Fig. 2. A full breakdown of the required classes and attributes can be found in [24].

4.4   Building a Data Request Result

After the DC implemented the proposed data model into its database system and received an authenticated DR for a DS, they can start the process to build the DR result.

First, the system selects all instances of the data set class that contain the identified and authenticated DS. Next, the selected data sets are checked for instances that contain other DS than the given DS in the data subject field as well.

In case another DS exists in the selection result, the system checks for the affection of the third party. If the rights and freedoms of the third party, namely the additional DSs, are affected, special care must be given. One option would be to drop this data set from the collected result, but this would make the DR response become incomplete. Including the data set could violate the rights and

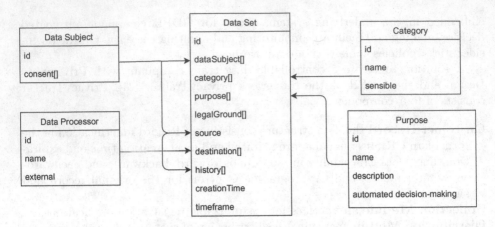

Fig. 2. Overview of classes and attributes in the data model

freedoms of the other DS. The best approach consists in performing a sufficient level of anonymization or pseudonymization, to overcome these issues, but feasibility of such is largely dependent on the type and information content of the concerned data set.

Otherwise, if no other DS's rights are affected, the system continues to check the next data set, until all are cleared. Afterwards, the references to the other classes in the data set are replaced with the respective values and the system checks, whether a purpose that includes automated decision-making is among the result. For each purpose concerned, an explanation of the logic involved and the possible implications for the DS is appended. This process is repeated for DPs that are tagged as external, with the safeguards for the data transfer to a non-EU entity appended instead. Finally, the result is transformed into the desired format and then forwarded to the DS.

The complete DR building process can be seen in Fig. 3. During the process, some complications exist. Creating an algorithm to automatically check data sets for affection of third parties is very challenging and strongly depends on the personal data in question. For example, scanning a picture for multiple, identifiable natural persons, requires a different technology and has other implications for the DSs, than having a home address, that is associated with multiple persons. How to determine that a third party is affected can also not be said unambiguously from the GDPR alone. Also, it is unclear how many DCs are facing this problem and which type of personal data are affected. Therefore, we do not give a general recommendation here. Instead, the DPO of the DC is advised to produce a concept for handling the data in question, depending on the personal data present. Thinkable approaches for handling these cases are determining the affection based on the category of personal data, or, as the WP29 recommends for data portability, find another legal ground to proceed [3].

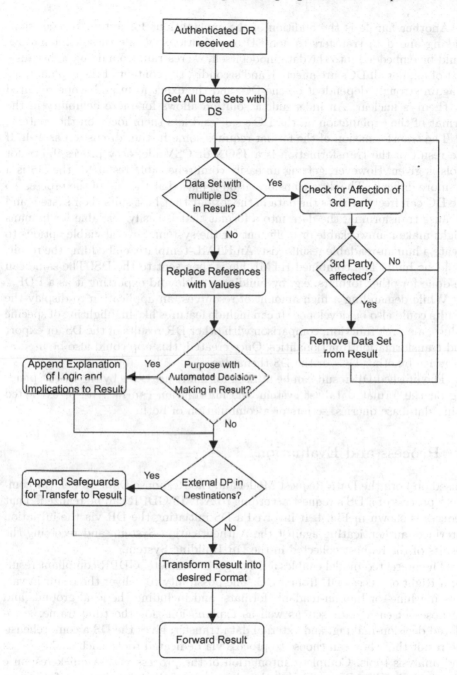

Fig. 3. Flowchart of data request creation process

Another hurdle is the addition of the explanations for automated decision-making and data transfers to non-EU organizations. While these explanations could be embedded into the data model itself, we restrain from doing so because, first of all, not all DCs are affected, and secondly, the content of the explanations is again strongly dependent on the DC, and the exact form and scope required for them is unclear. An independent solution allows for more flexibility in the format of the explanation on the DC's side and lets them focus on the content.

The transformation of the format requires some further discussion as well. If the result of the transformation is a JSON or CSV file, easy processibility for tools is given. However, getting an easily comprehensible result for the DS is a bit more difficult. The data transformation is placed at the end of the process, so the DC can freely process the data in the format that best suits their system and because transforming the data into a format that is easily readable for humans might make it unworkable or inefficient for the system. Several viable options to create a human-readable result exist. An HTML-template, embedding the result, could be built. The combined HTML file is then sent to the DS. The same can be done for other formats, e.g. by building a table and exporting it as a PDF.

While demanding a high amount of resources, an application to display the results could also be developed. It can include features like highlighting of specific values, a search function, comparison with other DR results of the DS, or export and transformation functionalities. Once created, this app could also be used as a service by other DCs or the DS themselves.

The finished DR result can be utilized for many use cases by the DS. Depending on the format database system, the information can be read or extracted using database queries, scripts or a combination of both.

5 Process and Evaluation

Based on both the Data Request Model and the Response Data Model, the complete process of a DS's request according to Art. 15 GDPR can be realized. That process is shown in Fig. 4. It involved a DS initiating the DR via the initiation interface, authenticating against the Authentication System, and receiving the results of the request collected in the DR Building System.

The presented model enables a DS to get a complete, GDPR compliant result for a Right of Access DR from a DC. The possibility to deliver the result in various machine- or human-readable formats, and including the legal grounds and purposes of each data set, as well as explanations for the time frame, automated decision-making, and external data transfer, gives the DS a comprehensible result that they can choose to process via dedicated tools, such as databases and analysis tools. Complete automation of the process with a quick response time is achievable. By restricting the placement of the initiation interface to an expected context the DS is granted increased accessibility. A secure authentication process can be achieved, e.g. based on multi-factor authentication, if such scheme is available to interact with the DS. For other scenarios, adequate best-fit alternatives have been discussed.

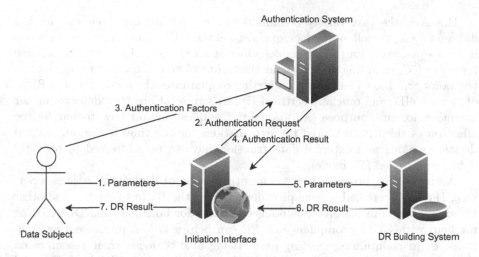

Fig. 4. Interactions between main components of data request model

The model consists of three separate components that can function independently from each other to fulfill their specific purpose. This allows a DC to potentially implement only one or two components, while developing an individual solution for the others. For the implementation of the model the DC has the flexibility to choose the solution best fit for their situation. Where applicable, existing solutions were outlined and discussed to aid in the selection process of the DC. Options to extend the model to include interfaces for other DS rights exist as well.

However, currently the model includes some open issues. The strict requirements for identity verification of the DS make it difficult for some DCs to implement a satisfactory authentication system. Especially DCs without access to user accounts and email addresses of the DS struggle to find enough secure authentication methods to build a secure identity verification scheme. To combat this, we encourage the further development of eID solutions and an IP system that promotes reliability and trustworthiness between all involved parties.

The other pressing issue is the undefined procedure to handle the affection of third parties, and the explanations for the time frame, automated decision-making, and external data transfers. These topics need to be researched further and have to be defined properly, so a general process, covering each scenario, can be developed for each of them.

6   Conclusion and Future Work

The generic data models and process for performing a Right of Access request according to Article 15 of the GDPR presented in this paper provide guidelines for both data controllers and data subjects concerning the implementation of a technical DR service. Based on legal and technical requirements, we provided both a Data Request Model for initiating a request and a Response Data Model for providing the requested data set, as well as a generic process for the overall interaction.

However, the vast variety of individual requirements and scenarios for the different DCs, as well as the lack of clarity of the GDPR on some aspects result in some open issues for the DR model. Offering a reliable and secure MFA scheme for every DC, including ones without the technical know-how and resources, is a key point that has to be worked on further to guarantee the security of the Right of Access. eIDs and officially certified IPs are two solutions that deserve further attention for this purpose. Additionally, the questions on how to handle the affection of third parties, and the explanations for the time frame, automated decision-making and external data transfers have to be addressed to properly define a universal DR model.

An interesting prospect is the conceptualisation of Right of Access as a Service. Having a certified service provider (SP) for the Right of Access and other DS rights functions as a reliable point of contact for both DSs and DCs looking for help with GDPR compliance. A SP can help a DC in implementing solutions, or in maintaining existing ones. Being able to focus their resources on the optimization of the DR process and their direct contact with both DSs and DCs also qualifies the SPs to look into the open issues and develop satisfying solutions. Especially for DCs that lack the technical or legal know-how to implement a GDPR compliant solution for the Right of Access and other DS rights themselves, having an officially recognized SP to aid with these problems is a key step towards guaranteeing DSs their rights. This makes Right of Access as a Service a worthwhile option to pursue, especially in the context of the data intermediaries as proposed in the European Data Governance Act. Similarly, the upcoming European Data Act will most likely impact on the requirements and implementation aspects of a Right of Access service as well.

References

1. Alizadeh, F., et al.: GDPR-reality check on the right to access data: claiming and investigating personally identifiable data from companies. In: Proceedings of Mensch Und Computer 2019, pp. 811–814 (2019)
2. Angulo, J., et al.: Usable transparency with the data track: a tool for visualizing data disclosures. In: Proceedings of the 33rd Annual ACM Conference Extended Abstracts on Human Factors in Computing Systems, Seoul, CHI 2015 Extended Abstracts, Republic of Korea, 18–23 April 2015, Begole, B. et al. (ed.), pp. 1803–1808. ACM (2015). https://doi.org/10.1145/2702613.2732701
3. ARTICLE 29 DATA PROTECTION WORKING PARTY 16/EN WP 242 rev.01 Guidelines on the right to data portability Adopted on 13 December 2016 As last Revised and adopted on 5 April 2017
4. Barrett, C.: Emerging trends from the first year of EU GDPR enforcement. Scitech Lawyer **16**(3), 22–35 (2020)
5. Basin, David, Debois, Søren., Hildebrandt, Thomas: On purpose and by necessity: compliance under the GDPR. In: Meiklejohn, Sarah, Sako, Kazue (eds.) FC 2018. LNCS, vol. 10957, pp. 20–37. Springer, Heidelberg (2018). https://doi.org/10.1007/978-3-662-58387-6_2
6. Blue, J., Furey, E.: A novel approach for protecting legacy authentication databases in consideration of GDPR. In: 2018 International Symposium on Networks, Computers and Communications (ISNCC), pp. 1–6. IEEE (2018)

7. Bozdag, E.: Data portability under GDPR: technical challenges. In: Available at SSRN 3111866 (2018)

8. Bray, T., et al.: The javascript object notation (json) data interchange format (2014)

9. Braz, C., Robert, J.M.: Security and usability: the case of the user authentication methods. In: Proceedings of the 18th Conference on l'Interaction Homme-Machine, pp. 199–203 (2006)

10. Brodin, M.: A framework for GDPR compliance for small-and medium-sized enterprises. Eur. J. Secur. Res. **4**(2), 243–264 (2019)

11. Bufalieri, L., et al.: GDPR: when the right to access personal data becomes a threat. In: 2020 IEEE International Conference on Web Services (ICWS), pp. 75–83. IEEE (2020)

12. Cagnazzo, M., Holz, T., Pohlmann, N.: GDPiRated – stealing personal information on- and offline. In: Sako, K., Schneider, S., Ryan, P.Y.A. (eds.) ESORICS 2019. LNCS, vol. 11736, pp. 367–386. Springer, Cham (2019). https://doi.org/10.1007/978-3-030-29962-0_18

13. Callas, J., et al.: Open PGP message format. Technical Report, RFC 2440, November 1998

14. De Hert, P., et al.: The right to data portability in the GDPR: towards user-centric interoperability of digital services. Comput. Law Secur. Rev. **34**(2), 193–203 (2018)

15. Di Martino, M., et al.: Personal information leakage by abusing the GDPR right of access. In: Fifteenth Symposium on Usable Privacy and Security (SOUPS 2019) (2019)

16. Vanberg, A.D., Ünver, M.B.: The right to data portability in the GDPR and EU competition law: odd couple or dynamic duo? Eur. J. Law Technol. **8**(1), 1–22 (2017)

17. Endorsement of GDPR WP29 guidelines by the EDPB. https://edpb.europa.eu/news/news/2018/endorsement-gdpr-wp29-guidelines-edpb_de. Accessed 24 Apr 21

18. European Commission. European data strategy - Making the EU a role model for a society empowered by data (2022). https://ec.europa.eu/info/strategy/priorities-2019-2024/Europe-fit-digital-age/european-data-strategy_en

19. Ferrara, P., Spoto, F.: Static analysis for GDPR compliance. In: ITASEC (2018)

20. Foster, I.D., et al.: Security by any other name: On the effectiveness of provider based email security. In: Proceedings of the 22nd ACM SIGSAC Conference on Computer and Communications Security, pp. 450–464 (2015)

21. Gjermundrød, H., Dionysiou, I., Costa, K.: privacyTracker: a privacy-by-design GDPR-compliant framework with verifiable data traceability controls. In: Casteleyn, S., Dolog, P., Pautasso, C. (eds.) ICWE 2016. LNCS, vol. 9881, pp. 3–15. Springer, Cham (2016). https://doi.org/10.1007/978-3-319-46963-8_1

22. Greze, B.: The extra-territorial enforcement of the GDPR: a genuine issue and the quest for alternatives. Int. Data Priv. Law **9**(2), 109–128 (2019)

23. Guamán, D.S., Del Alamo, J.M., Caiza, J.C.: GDPR compliance assessment for cross-border personal data transfers in android apps. IEEE Access **9**, 15961–15982 (2021)

24. Hansen, M.: Exploring a Universal Model for Data Requests per Article 15 of the GDPR. MA thesis. Kiel University of Applied Sciences, Germany (2021)

25. Herkenhöner, R., et al.: Towards automated processing of the right of access in inter-organizational web service compositions. In: 2010 6th World Congress on Services, pp. 645–652. IEEE (2010)

26. Huth, D.: A pattern catalog for GDPR compliant data protection. In: PoEM Doctoral Consortium, pp. 34–40 (2017)

27. Zulkarnain, S., Idrus, S., et al.: A review on authentication methods. Aust. J. Basic Appl. Sci. **7**(5), 95–107 (2013)
28. Karegar, F., Pulls, T., Fischer-Hübner, S.: Visualizing exports of personal data by exercising the right of data portability in the data track - are people ready for this?' In: Privacy and Identity Management. Facing up to Next Steps - 11th IFIP WG 9.2, 9.5, 9.6/11.7, 11.4, 11.6/SIG 9.2.2 International Summer School, Karlstad, Sweden, August 21-26, 2016, Revised Selected Papers. Lehmann, A., et al. (ed.) vol. 498. IFIP Advances in Information and Communication Technology, pp. 164–181 (2016). https://doi.org/10.1007/978-3-319-55783-0_12
29. Martin, Y.S., Kung, A.: Methods and tools for GDPR compliance through privacy and data protection engineering. In: 2018 IEEE European Symposium on Security and Privacy Workshops (EuroS&PW), pp. 108–111. IEEE (2018)
30. Ogriseg, C.: GDPR and personal data protection in the employment context. Labour Law Issues **3**(2), 1–24 (2017)
31. Pandit, H.J., O'Sullivan, D., Lewis, D.: GDPR data interoperability model. In: The 23rd EURAS Annual Standardisation Conference, Dublin, Ireland (2018)
32. Pavur, J., Knerr, C.: Gdparrrr: using privacy laws to steal identities. In: arXiv preprint arXiv:1912.00731 (2019)
33. Pearson, S., Casassa-Mont, M.: Sticky policies: an approach for managing privacy across multiple parties. Computer **44**(9), 60–68 (2011)
34. Powell, A., et al.: Understanding and explaining automated decisions. In: Available at SSRN 3309779 (2019)
35. Presthus, W., Sørum, H.: Consumer perspectives on information privacy following the implementation of the GDPR. Int. J. Inf. Syst. Proj. Manage. **7**(3), 19–34 (2019)
36. Presthus, W., Sørum, H., Andersen, L.R.: GDPR compliance in Norwegian Companies. In: Norsk konferanse for organisasjoners bruk at IT, vol. 26, no. 1 (2018)
37. Proposal for a REGULATION OF THE EUROPEAN PARLIAMENT AND OF THE COUNCIL on European data governance (Data Governance Act). COM/2020/767 final
38. Quermann, N., Degeling, M.: Data sharing in mobile apps—user privacy expectations in Europe. In: 2020 IEEE European Symposium on Security and Privacy Workshops (EuroS&PW), pp. 107–119. IEEE (2020)
39. Ramsdell, B., Turner, S.: Secure/multipurpose internet mail extensions (S/MIME) version 3.1 message specification. Technical Report, RFC 3851, July 2004
40. REGULATION (EU) 2016/679 OF THE EUROPEAN PARLIAMENT AND OF THE COUNCIL of 27 April 2016 on the protection of natural persons with regard to the processing of personal data and on the free movement of such data, and repealing Directive 95/46/EC (General Data Protection Regulation). OJ L 119, 4.5, pp. 1–88 (2016)
41. Shafranovich, Y.: Common format and MIME type for comma-separated values (CSV) files (2005)
42. Velásquez, I., Caro, A., Rodríguez, A.: Authentication schemes and methods: a systematic literature review. Inf. Softw. Technol. **94**, 30–37 (2018)
43. Wachter, S., Mittelstadt, B., Russell, C.: Counterfactual explanations without opening the black box: automated decisions and the GDPR. Harv. JL Tech. **31**, 841 (2017)

Can Authoritative Governments Abuse the Right to Access?

Cédric Lauradoux[✉]

University Grenoble-Alps, INRIA, Grenoble, France
cedric.lauradoux@inria.fr

Abstract. The right to access is a great tool provided by the GDPR to empower data subjects with their data. However, it needs to be implemented properly otherwise it could turn subject access requests against the subjects privacy. Indeed, recent works have shown that it is possible to abuse the right to access using impersonation attacks. We propose to extend those impersonation attacks by considering that the adversary has an access to governmental resources. In this case, the adversary can forge official documents or exploit copy of them. Our attack affects more people than one may expect. To defeat the attacks from this kind of adversary, several solutions are available like multi-factors or proof of aliveness. Our attacks highlight the need for strong procedures to authenticate subject access requests.

Keywords: Subject access right · Authentication · Impersonation · Forgery

1 Introduction

In 2011, Max Schrems, an Austrian citizen, sent a request to the US company Facebook[1] to access all the data held by the company. He received a huge PDF file (1200 pages) describing the data Facebook held on him. The analysis of the data shows that Facebook was not respecting European data protection laws. In 2018, David Caroll submitted a subject access request to UK company Cambridge Analytica. The company first refused to comply with Caroll's request, and it escalated until the UK data protection authority [13] asked the company to comply with Caroll's access request. In the end, Cambridge Analytica's actions during 2016's US election were exposed. In both cases, Facebook and Cambridge Analytica had to provide data to individuals in order to respect their right to access. In Europe, this right is defined in Article 15 of the GDPR. The right to access data is considered as the root for all the other rights defined by the GDPR. Once, a data subject has accessed the data collected by a data controller, he/she can exercise the other rights (to object, to data portability, to be forgotten, etc.).

The right to access needs to be implemented carefully to avoid data breaches. Indeed, an adversary can send a subject access request while impersonating a

---

[1] http://europe-v-facebook.org.

© Springer Nature Switzerland AG 2022
A. Gryszczyńska et al. (Eds.): APF 2022, LNCS 13279, pp. 23–33, 2022.
https://doi.org/10.1007/978-3-031-07315-1_2

legitimate subject to a data controller. If the data controller does not authenticate the access request properly, the adversary can obtain the data by abusing the right to access. This threat has to be considered seriously as data protections officers (DPOs) have already reported in [14] suspicious access requests. Researchers [6,8,9,14–16] have conducted studies to test if the right to access was implemented properly. They have used different strategies [8,9,15,16] to fool DPOs and succeeded to steal personal data in numerous cases. In response to those issues, the European Data Protection Board (EDPB) has recently published some guidelines [12] on the right of access to clarify its implementation and to improve the situation. Still many things have to be done to fix how subject access requests are handled by data controllers.

In this work, we focus on data controllers who authenticate a subject access request using an official document like an ID card or a passport. This authentication is often encountered in practice despite the fact that it can be irrelevant as pointed out in [6,12]. *We alert that there are more elaborated attacks possible if the adversary benefits from the support of a government.* In this case, the adversary can forge official document and impersonate any data subjects to forge subject access request. It allows authoritative or corrupted states to abuse the right to access to spy on dissidents who use online services eligible to subject access request. This kind of attacks needs to be avoided because it could clearly harm the reputation of the data protection regulations like the GDPR.

Official document forgery shows the limit of document-based authentication. Additional measures needs to be implemented by data controllers to prevent ID forgery. Multiple-factor authentication (MFA) is an interesting solution to thwart forgery attacks. *It requires that the data subject and the data controller agree on an additional secure communication (an electronic mail address or a phone number).*

The paper is organized as follows. Section 2 discusses how data controllers authenticate subject access requests. We describe the benefit of implementing the right to access using privacy dashboard or by DPOs. We review the existing attacks against the right to access in Sect. 3. We introduce our new attack scenarios in Sect. 4. Solutions are discussed in Sect. 5.

2   How are Subject Access Requests Authenticated?

The right to access one's personal data (Article 15 of GDPR [10]) via Subject Access Requests (SAR) is fundamental to ensure data protection. It makes the processing of personal data by organizations transparent and accountable towards data subjects, whereby these are made aware of, and can verify the lawfulness of the processing of their data (Recital 63 of GDPR [10]).

This right to access by individuals complements the mandate of the data protection authorities to monitor and enforce the application of the GDPR (Article 57.1.a of GDPR [10]). The right to access also enables the exercise of all the other rights (erasure, rectification, restriction, etc.). When a data controller receives an access request, it needs to perform two types of verification. A verification of the *eligibility* needs to be done. A data controller needs to verify if the subject sending a request is concerned by a data protection regulation which includes a right to access. A verification of the *legitimacy* needs also to be done by the data controller. Verifying the legitimacy has two purposes: i) establish the subject's identity, and ii) check that the subject's identity matches the requested data. Verifying both *eligibility* and *legitimacy* can be obtained by executing an appropriate authentication protocol between the data subject sending the access request and the data controller.

If no verification is implemented, the data of a subject can be collected by anyone impersonating the subject to the data controller. This is particularly demonstrated by Bufalieri *et al.* [8]. They submitted 334 subject access requests to different data controllers, and 58 organizations provided data without any verification of the subject sending the request. It confirms that the right to access without authentication is harmful to privacy. We discuss next how data controllers are actually handling subject access requests.

2.1 Dashboard Versus DPO

Two methods to handle subject access requests (see Fig. 1) have been implemented by data controllers. In the first method, a privacy dashboard has been implemented by the data controller. The subject authenticates to the controller's website and then can obtain his/her data or submit securely an access request to the controller's DPO. This solution has been chosen by Google or Facebook. They have created dashboard on their websites to let data subjects access their data. To access the dashboard, the data subject needs first to authenticate to the data controller websites. An extra verification may be required to obtain the data from the data controller as part as a two-factor authentication. Privacy dashboards are very convenient for the data subjects because the creation and the processing of their request is automatic. Google Takeout (https://takeout.google.com) is a good example of dashboard which implements two-factor authentication. More details on privacy dashboards can be found in [18].

In the second method, all the subject access requests are handled by the controller's DPO. The DPO is in charge of verifying both eligibility and legitimacy of the subject access requests. In this method, a first issue is to setup a secure communication channel to let the subject submits his/her request to the DPO. It can be done through a web page or by sending and electronic mail[2]. In any case, the communication channel between the subject and the DPO needs to be secure (using end-to-end encryption for instance). Once a secure channel has been setup, the DPO can interact with the subject to verify his/her request. It is important to notice that third parties can help the subject to contact the DPOs. A data protection authority can be contacted in the case for an indirect access. It can be also a third party which helps subjects to create their subject access requests like Tapmydata[3].

---

[2] Other more classical methods like postal mail are also available but they are not considered in this work.
[3] https://tapmydata.com.

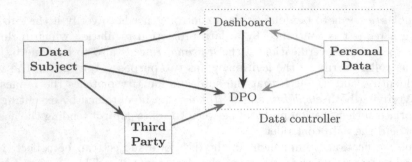

Fig. 1. Current options for the implementation of the right to access.

In Table 1, we compare the main characteristics of the different implementations one can come across. The security of the authentication scheme used in a dashboard is based on a secret shared (*i.e.* a password) between the data controller and the data subject. It is human-to-computer security mechanism based on the following assumptions: (i) the data subject does not share the secret with other individuals, (ii) the secret is not re-used to other data controllers, (iii) the secret is difficult to guess and (iv) the authentication is performed over secure channel. This technology is tried-and-tested even if it has some limitations [7].

Table 1. Comparison of the properties of the different implementations of the right to access.

	Dashboard	DPO
Creation of SAR	Automatic	Manual
Processing of SAR	Automatic/Manual	Manual
Security model	Password (+MFA)	Choice of the DPO

The authentication scheme implemented by DPO is a human-to-human interaction. It is based on the assumptions that: (i) the communication channels used between the subject and the DPO are secure, (ii) the data subject is the only individual able to prove that he/she has created his/her request and (iii) the DPO is trained to verify requests. The verification is a choice made by the DPO. This choice is critical to authenticate subject access requests. DPOs often ask the subject sending a request to provide a copy of an official identification document. This method of verification has been criticized in [12].

3   Threat Model and Known Attacks

A general threat model for the right to access was proposed by Boniface *et al.* [6]. This model considers both malicious subjects and malicious controllers, whereby three different categories of threats were defined: i) denial of access, ii) privacy invasion and iii) data breach due to impersonation. We briefly review denial of access and privacy invasion and then focus on data breach.

Denial of Access. This situation corresponds to cases in which data controllers decline to provide data to data subjects; one alleged reason refers to scenarios wherein they are not in a position to verify the identity of subjects.It also occurs often with companies collecting and processing cookies [6,11], but also with those processing IP addresses [4]. Denial of access was also observed in [5,6,11,19].

Privacy Invasion. This attack is defined in [6] as a case in which the data controller is honest-but-curious but requests additional information to authenticate the SAR. These additional requested information can increase the exposure of the subject to the controller and potentially violates the *minimization and proportionality principles* prescribing that personal data shall be is adequate, relevant and limited to what is necessary in relation to the purposes for which they are processed (Article 5 (1)(c) of the GDPR). For example, the controller should not be obliged to acquire additional information in order to identify the data subject for the sole purpose of being complaint (Recital 57 of the GDPR).

Data Breach. Data breach refers to the case of a data controller which provides the data of a given subject A to another subject B. A data breach can be the result of an error or it can be the result of an impersonation attack. Example of impersonation attacks against the right to access are given in [8,9,15,16]. These studies have demonstrated that it is possible to use the right of access to steal data by impersonating a data subject. Recent studies [8,9,15,16] show that data controllers are not ready to process correctly subject access requests because they still use weak authentication procedures vulnerable to impersonation attacks. Table 2 summarizes the different methods used to impersonate a subject and to abuse data controllers with illegitimate subject access requests. It is important to notice that the attacks were successful against data controllers which rely their DPOs to authenticate subject access requests.

4   Advanced Forgery Attacks

We demonstrate in this section that verification of subject access request based on official identification document can not resist to an adversary which is backup by a government. Indeed, we focus on DPOs who verify subject access requests by asking a copy of official identification document. Despite being criticized by EDPB in its guidelines [12], this method of verification is still considered valid depending on the information known by the data controller on the data subject. We assume that if the adversary is able to provide an official identification document then he/she can fool DPOs and therefore abuse the right to access. Other

Table 2. Known impersonation attacks abusing the right to access and their implementation.

Authentication method	Attacks	Target
Copy of an ID	Social engineering [16]	DPO
	Falsification [15]	DPO
Email confirmation	Email Spoofing [8,9,15]	DPO
Bills	Falsification [16]	DPO
Personal question	Social engineering [16]	DPO

authors (like [14] for instance) have made the same conclusion but they have not described scenarios and their impact as it is done in our work. Our attack is foreseen in three steps (as depicted in Fig. 2).

① The malicious state (represented by Charlie) needs first to identify the websites and services used by the target (Alice) located in the EU. He obtains the contact information of all the data controllers collecting and processing the data of their targets (including Bob).

② Charlie produces official documents (ID card, passport. . .) which match the identity of Alice. Charlie creates documents for a perfect namesake with the same first, last name, birth date, gender, etc. These documents are transmitted through a proxy (Eve).

③ Eve submits the subject access request to Bob and to any other controllers. Eve can provide valid government-issued documents whenever they are requested by data controllers.

④ Eve (and later Charlie) obtains Alice's data from Bob.

The first step is not mandatory. Indeed, Charlie and Eve can adopt a guess-and-determine strategy and submit subject access requests to many data controllers without knowing whether they collect and process personal data from Alice. If the data controller (Bob) answers, Charlie and Eve obtain Alice's data. However, this strategy is not particularly discreet and some data controllers may alert Alice that they have received strange requests.

The authoritative state may not necessarily need to use Eve as a proxy. Eve can be useful since she can be located in the same country as the targeted dissident: the request submitted by Eve would mimic the request that the target could have submitted.

Tools like the application Tapmydata[4] can simplify the task of the adversary. Tapmydata can be used to submit automatically requests to data controllers. It aims at simplifying the creation and the submission of subject access requests. As such, an adversary can register with an email address and confirm her identity by uploading a scanned of his/her forged passport. The application knows how to contact 1400 data controllers and takes care of all the administrative details

---

[4] https://tapmydata.com/.

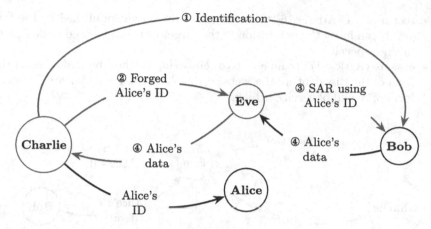

Fig. 2. Impersonation attack by an authoritative state (Charlie) against a dissident (Alice) using a proxy (Eve) to contact a data controller (Bob).

of the request. When a data controller replies to a request, the data is stored in a docker. In our context, it amplifies our attack.

A similar scenario can occur if an administrative who works in a department delivering official identification documents is corrupted. Figure 3 illustrates this case wherein Alice is a data subject using an online social network maintained by Bob (and located in the EU). Eve wants to obtain information on Alice. Eve knows that Charlie can be corrupted. Eve bribes Charlie to obtain the genuine identification document bearing Alice's information. Eve submits a SAR to Bob impersonating Alice. Eve can provide all the identification documents.

4.1 Impact Assessment

One may consider that this attack is unlikely to occur and that the adversary model is too strong. Governments have other legal means to access data from their citizens. Our attack scenario makes sens if we consider the case of dissidents and authoritative states. Let us assume that some dissidents are using online services located in Europe. The authoritative state they are against can use our forgery attack to abuse the right to access and spy on them. This scenario would demonstrate that the GDPR can be abused for surveillance purpose. Creating on-demand official identification documents and sending subject access requests are rather inexpensive. If the impersonation succeeds, there are two types of consequences:

- Direct consequences: a state can destabilize, denigrate or blackmail dissidents online.
- Indirect consequences: after a first impersonation attack, a state can further impersonate the target to exercise other rights (depending on its goal), for example:

- rectification (Article 16) to modify data or content published by the target. It can harm the reputation of the target or it can be used to denigrate his/her speech.
- erasure (Article 17) as an effective censorship method by removing all the data of the dissident from a website (his/her blog for instance). This is a form of denial of service attack.

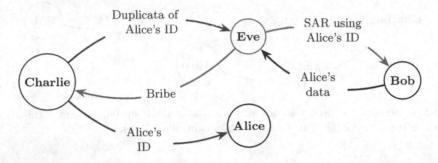

Fig. 3. Impersonation attack when an administrative Charlie is corrupted by Eve.

The scope of the GDPR increases the impact of our attack to more categories of people. First, we have dissidents who are using European online service. The authoritative state they are against can forge official identification documents at will and submit subject access request to data controllers which are in EU. Second, European citizen who have visited an authoritative state. The authoritative state can keep a copy of their passport when they cross the border during the customs check. The authoritative state can submit subject access requests to data controller anywhere who collect and process the data of the target. Third, Foreigners (Non European) who are using European online service who have visited an authoritative state. It demonstrates that an authoritative state can abuse the right to access and exploit the scope of the GDPR to reach as many people as possible.

4.2   Ethical Considerations

We have not implemented our attack due to ethical considerations. To his knowledge, the author does not collaborate with authoritative states. We have neither attempted to pay a bribe to an official. Even if our work is theoretical, the attack described is serious and could affect many data subjects.

5   Countermeasures

The verification made by the DPO to verify a request need to be relevant to the controller's knowledge of the data subject. Actually, document-based authentication can establish the identity of the subject securely even against governmental adversaries if three conditions are met:

1. The data controller knows the identity of the subject and an identifying element (picture of the face or another biometrics).
2. The data controller and the subject sending the request met physically.
3. The DPO is trained to verify official documents (passport or ID card).

It often fails because at least one of these conditions is not satisfied. If condition 3 is not verified, then an adversary can submit forged ID documents. The DPO needs to be trained to detect fake identification documents and document tampering. However, training DPOs is not enough to avoid attacks if a state is involved in the forgery of the ID documents. If the other conditions (1 and 2) are not verified, the patch is more costly.

Remote Identity Proofing – Let us assume that condition 2 cannot be satisfied, *i.e.* the DPO and the subject cannot met physically like in a police control. The DPO needs to use a remote identity proofing scheme as described in [2,3]. The verification can be done using a video call or pictures. It relies on a liveness check and authenticity check (see [2] for more details). it is important that the data controller knows both the identity and one biometrics of the subject before the verification. Otherwise a governmental adversary can succeed a forgery attack. If Bob knows only the identity of Alice, Charlie can forge a passport in the name of Alice with the picture and the biometrics of Eve. Eve can then impersonate Alice to Bob. Another approach for remote identity proofing is to rely on secure public electronic identification [1]. Such systems are considered for deployment in the European Union. They could be used straightforward to authenticate subject access requests sent by European residents. However, data controllers would need to find another method to authenticate requests from data subjects which are outside the European Union.

Multi-factor Authentication – MFA [17] is a solution to use if condition 1 cannot be satisfied. The DPO needs to consider all the information known on the subject to authenticate the subject's request. It can be a confirmation code sent on an email address or an SMS sent to a phone number for instance. It is important to notice that using a factor unknown by the controller before the request is not relevant and it cannot be trusted.

If the data controller needs strong authentication to interact with the subject, then the authentication mechanism can be re-used to verify subject access requests. Both data processing and exercise of the subjects right aligned. An important question rises if the data controller does not need strong authentication to process subjects data. Does the data controller need to implement strong authentication to verify subject access requests? If we consider the use of multi-factor authentication, a data controller can ask the subject to provide a phone number when he/she registers for the sole purpose of authenticating later subject access requests. Recital 64 of the GDPR states that *A controller should not retain personal data for the sole purpose of being able to react to potential requests.* The data controller needs to implement the data minimization principle during the verification. There is a conflict between the application of the minimization principle and the security of subject access requests. Asking additional data to the subject seems necessary to have a safe exercise of the right to access.

6 Conclusion

Governments have opportunities to abuse the right to access when a data controller authenticates subject access requests using only official identification documents. This form of authentication is particularly weak against forgery attacks. Dissidents who use online services proposed by European companies can be targeted by authoritative governments they oppose. The scope of the GDPR makes our attack reach more people than expected. Forgery attacks can be even obtained by corruption. If such attacks occur, these attacks would not only harm data subjects but they would also harm the trust on the personal data regulations like the GDPR.

Finding a solution is not simple because data controllers need to find the good trade-off between security and privacy. Implementing strong authentication using multiple factors mitigates the risks related to handling subject access requests. But the data controller may need to obtain more information like the subject phone number or an email address to implement multi-factor authentication. Such information may not need necessary for the controller's processing. It is hard to satisfy both the data minimization principle (Recital 64 of the GDPR) and a useful and secure right to access. Data protection authorities and board need to clarify if minimization or right to access prevails.

References

1. Privacy Features of European eID Card Specifications. Technical Report, ENISA, January 2009
2. Remote ID Proofing. Technical Report, ENISA, March 2021
3. Remote ID Proofing: Attacks & Countermeasures. Technical Report, ENISA, January 2022
4. Adhatarao, S., Lauradoux, C., Santos, C.: IP-based Subject Access Requests Denied (2021)
5. Ausloos, J., Dewitte, P.: Shattering one-way mirrors - data subject access rights in practice. Int. Data Priv. Law 8(1), 4–28 (2018)
6. Boniface, C., Fouad, I., Bielova, N., Lauradoux, C., Santos, C.: Security analysis of subject access request procedures. In: Naldi, M., Italiano, G.F., Rannenberg, K., Medina, M., Bourka, A. (eds.) APF 2019. LNCS, vol. 11498, pp. 182–209. Springer, Cham (2019). https://doi.org/10.1007/978-3-030-21752-5_12
7. Bonneau, J., Herley, C., van Oorschot, P.C., Stajano, F.: Passwords and the evolution of imperfect authentication. Commun. ACM 58(7), 78–87 (2015)
8. Bufalieri, L., Morgia, M.L., Mei, A., Stefa, J.: GDPR: when the right to access personal data becomes a threat. In: 2020 IEEE International Conference on Web Services, ICWS 2020, pp. 75–83. IEEE, Beijing, China, October 2020

9. Cagnazzo, M., Holz, T., Pohlmann, N.: GDPiRated – stealing personal information on- and offline. In: Sako, K., Schneider, S., Ryan, P.Y.A. (eds.) ESORICS 2019. LNCS, vol. 11736, pp. 367–386. Springer, Cham (2019). https://doi.org/10.1007/978-3-030-29962-0_18

10. Council of European Union: Council regulation (EU) no 2016/679 (2016). https://eur-lex.europa.eu/legal-content/EN/TXT/?uri=CELEX:32016R0679

11. Degeling, M., Utz, C., Lentzsch, C., Hosseini, H., Schaub, F., Holz, T.: We value your privacy...now take some cookies: measuring the GDPR's impact on web privacy. In: 26th Annual Network and Distributed System Security Symposium, NDSS 2019, The Internet Society, San Diego, California, USA, February 2019. https://arxiv.org/abs/1808.05096

12. European Data Protection Board: Guidelines 01/2022 on data subject rights - Right of access. Technical Report, January 2022. https://edpb.europa.eu/our-work-tools/documents/public-consultations/2022/guidelines-012022-data-subject-rights-right_en

13. Information Commissioner's Office: Enforcement Notice. Technical Report, 2258812, ICO (2018). https://ico.org.uk/media/action-weve-taken/enforcement-notices/2258812/en-scl-elections-20180504.pdf

14. Martino, M.D., Meers, I., Quax, P., Andries, K., Lamotte, W.: Revisiting identification issues in GDPR 'Right Of Access' policies: a technical and longitudinal analysis. In: Privacy Enhancing Technologies, PETS 2022. Lecture Notes in Computer Science, vol. 8555, Springer (To appear 2022)

15. Martino, M.D., Robyns, P., Weyts, W., Quax, P., Lamotte, W., Andries, K.: Personal information leakage by abusing the GDPR 'Right of Access'. In: Fourteenth Symposium on Usable Privacy and Security (SOUPS), pp. 371–386. ACM, USENIX Association, Santa Clara, CA, USA, August 2019

16. Pavur, J.: GDPArrrrr: using privacy laws to steal identities. In: Blackhat USA, Arxiv, Las Vegas, NV, USA (2019). https://arxiv.org/abs/1912.00731

17. van Tilborg, H.C.A., Jajodia, S. (eds.): Multifactor Authentication, pp. 808–808. Springer, US (2011). https://doi.org/10.1007/978-1-4419-5906-5

18. Tolsdorf, J., Fischer, M., Lo Iacono, L.: A case study on the implementation of the right of access in privacy dashboards. In: Gruschka, N., Antunes, L.F.C., Rannenberg, K., Drogkaris, P. (eds.) APF 2021. LNCS, vol. 12703, pp. 23–46. Springer, Cham (2021). https://doi.org/10.1007/978-3-030-76663-4_2

19. Urban, T., Tatang, D., Degeling, M., Holz, T., Pohlmann, N.: A study on subject data access in online advertising after the GDPR. In: Pérez-Solà, C., Navarro-Arribas, G., Biryukov, A., Garcia-Alfaro, J. (eds.) DPM/CBT -2019. LNCS, vol. 11737, pp. 61–79. Springer, Cham (2019). https://doi.org/10.1007/978-3-030-31500-9_5

Security of Personal Data

The Data Protection Implications of the EU AML Framework: A Critical Overview & the Case of AI

Iakovina Kindylidi[1,2](✉)

[1] NOVA School of Law, 1099-032 Lisbon, Portugal
imk@vda.pt
[2] Vieira de Almeida & Associados, 1200-151 Lisbon, Portugal

Abstract. The tension and the need for alignment between the data protection and AML/CFT framework has been pointed out by scholars and authorities since the first AMLD, over thirty years ago. Despite the criticism, none of the competent authorities has issued a pragmatic guidance aiming at consolidating the two regimes. This lack of regulatory clarity together with the fragmented implementation and interpretation of the AMLD across the EU are aggravating the challenges of the obliged entities. At the same time, the adoption of emerging technologies, such as AI for AML/CFT purposes, is further highlighting the need for harmonising the various conflicting obligations to avoid duplication and gold-plating practices. Following a doctrinal approach of primary sources, the present aims to contribute to the discussion towards a reconciliation between the data protection and AML/CFT framework from the perspective of the obliged entities, considering the recent regulatory developments, namely the AML Package and the AIA Proposal, the relevant case law of the EUCJ, and the current literature.

Keywords: AML · Data protection · AI

1 Introduction

The tension and, concomitantly, the need for alignment between the data protection and anti-money laundering (AML)/counter-terrorist financing (CFT) framework has been pointed out since the first anti-money laundering Directive (AMLD), over thirty years ago. However, although more recently European authorities, such as Article 29 Working Party (WP29) [1], the European Data Protection Board (EDPB) [14, 15] the European Data Protection Supervisor (EDPS) [16, 17] and the European Banking Authority (EBA) [7], have been underlining the need for coherent interpretation and consolidation of the two regimes, none of them has issued concrete guidance on the matter. In this regard, together with the fact that, so far, the AML/CFT matters were regulated via Directives, an inconsistent implementation and interpretation of the AML/CFT framework across the EU and amongst obliged entities has been noted [14, p. 6].

At the same time, the literature in the topic is rather limited [4, 22, 23], focusing mostly on the data protection challenges of data sharing and data accessibility by the

© Springer Nature Switzerland AG 2022
A. Gryszczyńska et al. (Eds.): APF 2022, LNCS 13279, pp. 37–49, 2022.
https://doi.org/10.1007/978-3-031-07315-1_3

Financial Investigation Units (FIUs) [5, 20, 24] and not addressing the data protection issues faced by obliged entities.

Moreover, as the adoption of Artificial Intelligence (AI) systems for AML/CFT purposes by obliged entities is increasing exponentially, the data protection and regulatory challenges are becoming more complex and the need for pragmatic guidance that allows for consistent and complimentary obligations of the obliged entities is pertinent.

In light of the above, the present will try to contribute to the discussion towards a reconciliation between the data protection and AML/CFT framework from the perspective of the obliged entities, considering the recent regulatory developments, namely the Proposals for an AI Regulation (AIA Proposal or AIA) [10] and for an AML Regulation (AML Proposal) [12]. Following a doctrinal analysis of primary sources and taking into consideration, where relevant, the case law of the European Court of Justice (EUCJ), an overview of the AML/CFT framework and its challenges (Sect. 2) will be presented while focusing on specific data protection issues (Sect. 3). Finally, the additional data protection and regulatory concerns when AI systems are used for AML/CFT purposes will be discussed (Sect. 4), while some suggestions for defusing the tension between the different frameworks will be presented (Sect. 5).

For clarity it should be noted that any reference to AMLD refers to Directive (EU) 2015/849, as amended, including the latest amendments brought by Directive (EU) 2018/843 (5th AMLD), except if stated otherwise. Any reference to AI should be understood as referring only to machine learning, including deep learning AI, while the terms AI or algorithm or AI system are used interchangeably. Lastly, data protection issues related to the disclosure and processing of personal data by the FIUs or other national competent authorities will not be addressed.

2   AML/CTF Framework: An Overview of the Challenges

The objective and core function of AMLD, since the first anti-money laundering Directive in 1990, is to prevent the use of the financial system for the purposes of money laundering (ML) or terrorist financing (TF) across the EU. The obligations posed to the obliged entities of Article 2 AMLD are following a risk-based case-by-case analysis of the particular customer and transaction. The premise of this risk-based approach is that the risks of ML or TF are not the same and, as such, the obliged entities should use an evidence-based decision-making process to determine the extent and nature of the measures that they put in place (Recital 22 and Article 13(2)).

To assess the level of risk, irrespective of the monitoring activities carried, AMLD requires the collection and processing of numerous personal data of customers in a timely manner (Recital 16), while ensuring that this information is up-to-date. This data can be collected from various sources, including public registries, directly from the customer or from other reliable sources. The objective of this processing is the identification of persons engaged in criminal activities while ensuring the maximum integrity of such process.

More specifically, the obliged entities should carry in certain circumstances Customer Due Diligence (CDD) (Article 11). As an ongoing process, CDD starts from onboarding and establishing a relationship with the client, including Know Your Customer (KYC), and extends throughout the business relationship (Article 13). Depending on a risk-based assessment carried by the obliged entities, more invasive due diligence activities may be put in place. For instance, obliged entities may need to carry an Enhanced Due Diligence (EDD), in case of transactions involving high-risk third countries identified pursuant to Article 9(2) (Articles 18 and 18a). In such situations, the customer may be required to provide additional information, including personal data, without being informed about the purposes of such further monitoring activities.

Although AMLD is descriptive of the measures that the obliged entities should put in place and the objective of the information collection, such as identifying the customer and other relevant individuals and their business profiles (Recital 31 and Article 13), it does not specify the types of information that the obliged entities should process to comply with their CDD obligations,[1] while it does not refer in detail to the processing of special categories of personal data, including data relating to criminal convictions and offences. Moreover, although the EBA has issued over the years a series of practical recommendations for compliance with the AMLD, including the recent revision of its Risk-Based Supervision Guidelines [7], it has not issued guidance on the matter of information that should be collected by customers. Similarly, there is little to no guidance from the Financial Action Task Force (FATF) on the matter.[2]

Moreover, aggravating factors have been the lack of harmonisation amongst the Member States allowing for significant differences amongst Member States, the AML/CFT measures deployed by obliged entities and the data collection practices followed.[3] In addition to the fact that a directive has been chosen as the regulatory vehicle so far for regulating AML/CFT matters, several provisions of AMLD allow derogations by the Member States. In particular, Article 7(1) states that each Member State should identify, assess, understand and mitigate risks related to data protection. Although the provision was firstly introduced when Directive 95/46/EC was still in force, it should be noted that the first paragraph of Article 7 has not been amended by the 5th AMLD. Similarly, Member States are able to determine which data is considered useful and proportionate to gather by the obliged entities to meet their AML/CFT obligations (Recital 21 of 5th AMLD). Finally, AMLD states that the retention period should not exceed five (5) years from the end of the business relationship or occasional transaction, however, the Member States can further extend it, for no more than five (5) years, pursuant to their own risk-assessment (Article 40 and Recital 21 5th AMLD). Taking into consideration

---

[1] Without prejudice to the data identified in relation to beneficiary owners in Article 30 AMLD (i.e. date of birth and contact details) and the information contained in central registries by the Member States, pursuant to Article 32a AMLD.

[2] Interestingly so, aside from a general reference to complying with the data protection requirements, such as data localisation and security, FATF in its AML/CFT Guidance and Methodologies, when it comes to data protection it only expressly refers to the confidentiality and data protection obligations of competent authorities [18, p. 111; 19, p. 93].

[3] Similar observation has been made by FATF in its Methodology for Assessing Technical Compliance with FATF Recommendations and the Effectiveness of AML/CFT Systems [18, p. 22].

the fragmented implementation across the EU and the concerns expressed by obliged entities operating in more than on Member State, EBA, in its Risk Based Supervision Guidelines, pointed out that there is some legal uncertainty around personal data processing for AML/CFT due to these powers of the Member States and has requested further guidance from the European Commission (EC) [16, p. 73].

At the same time, although the objective of the risk-based approach is to increase efficiency in combating ML and TF across the EU Single Market, over the years a perverse effect has been noted: obliged entities, due to the lack of specific guidance as to the measures that should be implemented and the data that should be collected, to avoid possible fines and demonstrate compliance with their AMLD obligations instead of following a case-by-case analysis of risks they are implementing one-size-fits-all solutions; a phenomenon that the WP29 referred to as 'gold-plating' [1, p. 3; 22, p. 14]. Of course, such problematic behaviour is undermining the objective of the risk-based approach of AMLD, and, ultimately, is posing serious threats to fundamental rights, including privacy, since it is clearly against the principle of proportionality and data minimisation.

In order to address some of the issues relating to the lack of harmonisation across the EU, the EC recently published its AML Package (the Package). The Package contains for the first time a Proposal for an AML Regulation, aiming to provide a single rulebook for AML/CFT, applicable throughout the EU. A Regulation is expected to provide to the obliged entities operating across the EU some level of legal clarity and security, while reducing compliance-associated costs. In addition, the AML Proposal is complemented by a Proposal for a Directive (so called the 6th AMLD) [9] focusing on the activities of the national supervisory authorities and the FIUs. The analysis of the latter exceeds the scope of the present.

Already in its Communication for an Action Plan, the EC had highlighted the importance of ensuring that processing activities and sharing of data between obliged entities and authorities is compliant with the data protection framework [8, p. 6]. In that respect, the AML Proposal is entrusting the AML Authority (AMLA) to prepare, amongst others, draft regulatory technical standards on CDD which will contain a minimum set of information that the obliged entities should collect before entering into new business relationships or in order to assess their existing ones, following a risk assessment for each customer/transaction (Recital 41 and Articles 18 and 20). If implemented correctly, gold-plating practices, including excessive collection of personal data can be minimised.

Although some specific provisions regarding data protection of the AML Proposal will be addressed in the respective chapters below,[4] it should be noted that the AML Proposal is also referring to another complex data protection issue following the recommendations from the EDPS [17] and the EDPB on the matter [14]; international data transfers between obliged entities of the same group that are situated in third countries that do not provide adequate levels of data protection (Article 14). Although the wording

---

[4] *See* Sect. 3 below regarding processing of certain categories of data and Sect. 4 regarding outsourcing.

proposed takes into consideration the latest developments following the Schrems II decision of the EUCJ,[5] it is preferable that the issuance of guidelines on the matter is not left solely on AMLA, but it is developed in collaboration with the EDPB. Furthermore, the AML Proposal is reinstating the five (5) year retention period, removing the problematic provision that allowed the Member States to extent the retention period (Article 56).

Lastly, it should be highlighted that although the EDPS has welcomed the AML Proposal, it considers that certain data protection issues remain in the current wording of the draft [16, pp. 16–18]. In the following Sect. 1 will analyse some of these topics, taking into account, where relevant, the approach followed in the AML Proposal.

3 Specific Data Protection and AML Challenges

3.1 AML Data Protection Provisions

Section 5 AMLD includes some data protection provisions, however, it fails to provide guidance to obliged entities on data collection practices. More specifically, in addition to the data retention provisions referred above (Article 40), Article 41 (2) AMLD mandates that the personal data processed for the purposes of AML/CFT shall not be further processed in any way that is incompatible to such purposes, while it should not be processed for commercial purposes.

Although the EDPB has not issued specific recommendations regarding the interplay between AML and GDPR, in its Guidelines regarding the convergence between GDPR and PSD2 it states that further processing will only be possible when the data subject has given consent, pursuant to Article 6(1)(a) GDPR, or the processing is laid down by Union law or Member State law to which the controller is subject. Outside of these cases "the compatibility test of Article 6(4) GDPR cannot result in a legal basis for processing" [13, p. 11].[6] In any case, the prohibition of processing for commercial purposes, may prove problematic when it comes to further processing activities carried by service providers contracted by the obliged entity, especially in relation to processing of data related to criminal convictions and offences.[7]

Moreover, although the processing activities carried by the obliged entities could be considered necessary for compliance with the legal obligations posed under the AMLD (Article 6(1) lit.c.), the obliged entities should, in any case, provide sufficient information to the individuals pursuant to Articles 13 GDPR, before establishing a business relationship or carrying out an occasional transaction (Article 41(3)). In practice, of course, such information is usually included in lengthy wrap contracts of the obliged entities, making doubtful whether the individual has been duly informed. Additionally, Article 45 mandates the obliged entities to include and develop data protection and data sharing policies for AML/CFT purposes. In line with Sect. 1 above, there is no guidance by any

---

[5] C-311/18 - Facebook Ireland and Schrems, available https://curia.europa.eu/juris/liste.jsf?num=C-311/18.

[6] The same conclusion is drawn by the EDPB regarding silent party data. In this regard, note that PSD2 states that data collected should only be used for the purpose of providing the requested services.

[7] See Sect. 3 below.

European authority on the minimum context of such policies. This is one of the points that the AML Proposal is aiming to address, by tasking the AMLA to prepare regulatory standards regarding the minimum requirements of such policies (Recital 28 and Article 7(4)). Similar to the point made above, considering the nature of such guidance, it is necessary that the EDPB and EDPS meaningfully contribute in the elaboration of these guidelines.

3.2 Processing of Certain Categories of Personal Data for AML/CFT Purposes

Obliged entities are expressly allowed to process sensitive data, including data related to criminal convictions and offences for AML/CFT purposes. However, as mentioned in Sect. 1, AMLD does not include specific guidance on the matter.

According to Article 10 GDPR, the processing of personal data related to criminal convictions is heavily restricted and can only be carried under the control of official authority or if authorised by Union or Member State law which should provide for appropriate safeguards for the rights and freedoms of individuals. It should be noted that according to EUCJ,[8] data related to criminal convictions and offences are subject to the restrictions of Article 10 GDPR, even if it is collected from publicly accessible and non-official sources, such as newspapers or online pages.

Contrary to AMLD, for the first time, the AML Proposal is specifically addressing the processing of special categories of data referred in Article 9(1) GDPR and of data relating to criminal convictions and offences (Article 55). Moreover, it is setting out specific safeguards for such processing, while maintaining the general principle prohibiting further processing of data for purposes incompatible to AML/CFT and processing for commercial purposes. The safeguards include an obligation to dully inform customers about the collection of such data and the purpose for such collection, to ensure that the data come from reliable sources, is accurate and up-to-date and to put in place sufficient technical and organisational measures pursuant to Article 32 GDPR. Additionally, for data related to criminal convictions and offenses, in line with the data minimisation principle and as recommended by EDPB [14, p. 6], only data related to ML and its predicate offences, and TF can be collected, while the obliged entities are mandated to distinguish between allegations, investigations, proceedings and convictions, taking into consideration the right to fair trial, right of defence and presumption of innocence.

Although the provision should be welcomed, there is need for further guidance, firstly, as to what will be considered a reliable source. Many screening services offered by third-party service providers to obliged entities usually combine data coming from publicly available, non-official sources,[9] such as via media scrapping. EDPS has recommended that in any case the customers should be informed about the use and type (public/non-public) of external sources for the purposes of CDD. In this regard, EDPS proposed that the circumstances under which third party sources can be used should be clarified following also a risk-based approach [16, p. 13]. In any case, when watchlists are used the obliged entities should verify the sources and the accuracy of such information and should not base their decision solely on such information.

---

[8] *See* among others, Case C-136/17, C.G, CURIA - Documents (europa.eu).

[9] Watchlists as refereed in the Letter of the EBPD [14, p. 5].

Moreover, it should be clarified, in a non-exhaustive list, which offenses should be considered predicate offences of ML to avoid (yet again) fragmented enforcement across the EU. Closely related to this, in relation to differentiating between convictions and allegations, even if it accepted that the employee or manager of the obliged entity has the capacity to recognise and assess the differences between the various stages of a criminal process, it is highly doubtful that the decision of the obliged entity will not be affected by allegations against the customer, considering especially the risk-averse approach of the financial sector.

Finally, and pursuant to the data minimisation and proportionality principle, EDPS further recommended to specify which special categories of data of Article 9(1) can be processed by obliged entities, prohibiting the processing of personal data related to sexual orientation or ethnic origin of the customer [16, p. 10]. Even if such explicit wording is not included in the final text of the AML Regulation, it is advised that such clarification is included in the AMLA guidelines identifying the types of data that should be collected by the obliged entities based on the risk circumstances.

3.3 Proportionality and Risk-Assessment

Article 43 AMLD expressly states that AML/CFT purposes should be considered to be matters of public interest under GDPR. However, as it is underlined in Recital 34 of the 5th AMLD, a balance should be stricken between the public interest in the prevention of ML and TF and the fundamental rights of individuals, including their privacy. Although Recital 34 and Article 31 respectively refer to beneficial owners, the principle should extend to all the processing activities carried for AML/CFT purposes. This is also in line with the general principle of AMLD stating that it respects "the fundamental rights and observes the principles recognised by the Charter of Fundamental Rights of the European Union…in particular…the right to the protection of personal data (Article 8 of the Charter) …" (Recital 51 5th AMLD).

Therefore, pursuant to the risk-based approach embedded in AMLD, the obliged entities should assess whether and to what extent the measures they deploy for meeting their obligations are proportionate and respect the right to data protection of the individual. Such assessment can be carried in the context of a Data Protection Impact Assessment (DPIA). It should be noted that even in the case of outsourcing of CDD activities, the obliged entity, as a data controller, will be responsible for the DPIA, although it can request assistance from the service provider, especially when emerging technologies such as AI are used.[10]

Considering the amount of data or the sensitive nature of the information processed in the course of CDD activities as well as the restrictions posed to the rights and freedoms of the individuals, particularly when their personal information is disclosed to third parties and competent authorities or in the case of EDD, it is reasonable to consider processing for AML/CFT as high-risk processing under Article 35 GDPR. Thus, a DPIA would be required.

WP29, in its DPIA Guidelines [3, pp. 9–11], developed rules regarding the concept of high-risk operations and divided the GDPR criteria of Article 35 into nice (9) further

---

[10] *See* Sect. 4 below.

sub-criteria. According to WP29, if 2 out of the 9 sub-criteria are fulfilled, a DPIA is likely needed. One of the criteria is processing activities that evaluate or score, amongst others, the economic situation, reliability or behaviour or an individual (Recitals 71 and 91 GDPR). As an example of such activity, screening by a financial institution for AML/CFT or fraud is explicitly mentioned (Article 29 Working Party 2017, 9). Without prejudice to other criteria such as large scale processing or matching and combining datasets that may be met depending on the particular processing activities and AML/CFT methods deployed, AML/CFT processing activities clearly meet the fourth criterion set by WP29 regarding processing involving sensitive data, such as data regarding individuals' political opinions (Article 9(1)), as in the case of politically exposed persons (PEPs), as well as data related to criminal convictions or offences. Finally, the ninth WP29's criterion will also be met, since the processing activity may exclude or prevent an individual from using a service or contract. Again, in this case, WP29 uses as an example screening carried by financial institutions [3, p. 11]. It should be noted that in addition to the criteria established by GDPR and by WP29, DPAs may also set up lists of activities that require DPIA.

The minimum content of a DPIA is outlined in Article 35(7) GDPR. In any case, the obliged entities should clearly outline their processing activities, map and assess the severity and likelihood of the risks posed by the processing to the rights and freedoms of the individuals, as well as provide for suitable and specific technical and organisational measures to safeguard the fundamental rights and the interests of the data subject. When the risks are particularly high, prior consultation with the competent data protection authority may be necessary (Article 36 GDPR). In the case of AML/CFT processing, it has been proposed that such prior consultation is made mandatory [22, p. 24].

4 AI-Based AML/CFT Solutions: Raising the Stakes

4.1 Outsourcing and Article 22 GDPR

AMLD does not regulate the use of service providers for CDD activities. On the contrary, the AML Proposal states that an obliged entity can outsource the CDD activities, except if the service provider is established in a high-risk third country, is considered to have compliance weaknesses or is posing a threat to the financial system of the EU (Recital 62 and Article 40).

Although the AML Proposal does not refer to specific technologies, AI-based AML/CFT solutions are widespread promoting a time- and cost-efficient CDD. Irrespective of their level of automation and sophistication, service providers are offering series of AML/CFT services, such as KYC, identification of PEPs and transaction monitoring, amongst others.

Usually, AI-providers, either to provide their services or to further train their models or develop relevant databases, but in any case, in the course of providing their services, are collecting, processing and storing data that may not be relevant or necessary for the purposes of AML/CFT, such as geolocation, behavioural and even biometric data. Thus, this exponential use of AI solutions and outsourcing AML/CFT obligations is exacerbating the data protection related risks for individuals and is escalating the tension between AML and GDPR.

Of course, pursuant to AMLD and irrespective of whether outsourcing the AML/CFT obligations will constitute a critical or important activity pursuant to the EBA Outsourcing Guidelines [6], the obliged entity remains entirely responsible for compliance with the AML/CFT requirements.[11] This would mean that again a risk-based approach, tailored to the risk profile of the customer/transaction should be followed. However, this may prove complicated or even impossible to implement considering that many obliged entities are acquiring off-the-shelf AI solutions. From a GDPR perspective, the obliged entity, as the data controller for the processing activities in the AML/CFT context, will be liable for the processing carried.

Moreover, the use of AI AML/CFT solutions makes necessary the analysis of such processing in the light of Article 22 GDPR. Article 22 GDPR restricts data processing operations when they entail "a decision based solely on automated processing" including, but not limited to, profiling when it "produces legal effects concerning the data subject or similarly significantly affects the data subject".

The concept of "based solely on automated decision" implies that the power to make a decision rests solely in the AI system. In other words, if the person supervising the AI does not have the power to override or understand it's functioning in a manner that would allow error detection and correction, Article 22 GDPR is applicable. Although this may vary depending on the specific AI solution, for the purposes of the present it is considered that the processing carried by an AI-based AML/CFT solution will be based solely on automated means, since in most cases, even if the obliged entity is able to define some characteristics of the system and adapt it to its risk appetite, internal policies or the applicable national law and regulators recommendations, the human involvement will not be sufficient for the process to fall out of the scope of Article 22.

In relation to the second criterion of Article 22, an AML AI system should be considered that it is used to produce legal effects concerning an individual or that it will similarly significantly affect them. According to WP29's Guidelines on automated decision-making, a decision should be considered as having legal effects concerning the individuals when it affects a person's legal rights, legal status or rights under a contract. Moreover, to assess whether there are significantly similar effects, WP29 establishes three (3) criteria: the processing (a) to significantly affect the circumstances, behaviour or choices of the individuals concerned; (b) to have a prolonged or permanent impact on the data subject; or (c) at its most extreme, to lead to the exclusion or discrimination of individuals [2, p. 21]. Again, although the specific characteristics of an AI-system should be analysed to determine whether any of these criteria are met, Recital 71 GDPR points also to this direction when using the example of "automatic refusal of an online credit application". Similar examples are mentioned by WP29 ([2, p. 21].

Furthermore, Article 22 expressly outlines the three (3) possible legal basis for automated decision making: (a) processing is necessary for entering into or performance of contract; (b) processing is authorised by Union or Member State law, provided that such law lays down suitable measures to safeguard data subject's rights, freedoms and legitimate interests, and (c) data subject's explicit consent. Therefore, for obliged entities, automated decision making for AML/CFT can be used to assist them meeting their legal obligations under AMLD.

---

[11] Similarly, in the AML Proposal (Recital 62 and Article 40(1)).

In light of the above, the obliged entities should meet the obligations posed to data controllers using automated-decision making, including the obligation to provide necessary information. WP29 suggests, as a good practice and to ensure a fair processing, that the following information is provided when AI is used to carry out the processing of data, irrespective of whether the processing falls within the scope of Article 22 or not [2, pp. 24–24]: (a) Inform individuals about engaging in automated-decision making or profiling; (b) Provide meaningful information about the logic involved, and (c) Explain the significance and foreseen consequences of such processing. This information, depending on the processing activity, should be provided together with the specific information outlined in Articles 13 and 14 GDPR. Although it exceeds the scope of the present, it should be noted that in addition to an ex ante obligation to provide the information outlined above, a vivid academic debate had ensued on whether there is also an obligation of an ex post explanation for any processing activity involving AI [21, 25]. If such obligation is considered to exist, it will also impact the scope of the transparency obligations of the obliged entities under the GDPR.

In addition to what is stated in Sect. 3 regarding DPIA, since the risks for the right and freedoms of the individuals are elevated when AI systems are used (Article 35(3) lit. a GDPR), the need for a DPIA is increased. This is also in line with WP29 DPIA Guidelines [3, p. 22]. Even if the technology is being assessed, the obliged entity as data controller will remain responsible for the DPIA on the implementation of the technology. For such purposes, the AI-provider can assist by providing the necessary information or even complimenting the obliged entity's DPIA with its own. This information can extend to data management of training and testing datasets mandated by high-risk AI-providers, as it will be analysed below.

Lastly, it should be noted that the AML Proposal is further requesting AMLA to develop suitable guidelines and conditions regarding outsourcing, including criteria for compliance assessment (Recital 63 and Article 41 AML Proposal). Such step should be welcomed. However, considering that more and more AI solutions are deployed by obliged entities for combating ML and TF, AMLA should make a pragmatic and specific reference to AI-providers, aligned with the AIA, once finalised. In that sense, such AI-systems should be clearly classification based on their risk level.

4.2 AIA Proposal

In addition to the above, it is important to assess and align possible risks and obligations for the obliged entities in light of the AIA Proposal. High-risk AI systems are identified as those that "have a significant harmful impact on the health, safety and fundamental rights of persons in the Union", including for the protection of personal data (Recitals 27 and 28 AIA Proposal). Moreover, Recital 37 states that AI systems for assessing credit score or creditworthiness of natural persons, at least when not just used by small-scale providers, should be considered as high-risk, since they may determine the financial resources of the person or prolong discriminatory practices. In this regard, it is interesting to note that the AIA Proposal is indeed taking into consideration both the use of AI by financial institutions as well as the need to require such AI systems as high risk (Recital 80). Therefore, although not expressly referring to AML/CFT systems, it is reasonable to consider such AI-systems as high-risk, covered by category 5.lit (b) of Annex III of the

AIA Proposal. This means that providers and users of such systems should comply with the high-risk AI obligations.

Although most of the obligations of high-risk AI systems are posed to AI providers, there is a series of monitoring and reporting as well as data quality control obligations posed to AI users of such systems (Article 29). Notwithstanding, it should be noted that under the AIA Proposal any of the stakeholders involved in the AI value chain may be considered a provider and, therefore, it will be required to comply with the corresponding obligations, when putting a system in the market or into service under their name or trademark, modifying its purpose or making substantial adaptions to an AI system (Article 28). This may prove particularly important for obliged entities using AI systems for AML/CFT purposes and it should be a criterion for determining whether to contract a specific AI provider.

Amongst the elements that should be taken into consideration when selecting an AI provider should be the sources of the data used for the training, verification and testing process of high-risk AI systems. Considering the analysis in Sect. 3 regarding the doubtful accuracy of watchlists for screening purposes, it is advised that the obliged entities require from the AI-providers not only information about the conformity assessment of their system under AIA but also information on the data governance and management practices for the training and testing datasets in line with Article 10 AIA Proposal.

5   Conclusion: Resolving the Tension

In light of the above, it is evident that the interplay between AMLD, GDPR and AIA is not clearly and coherently addressed. To increase the efficiency of the existing and upcoming AML/CFT rules, their adoption by the industry and their enforceability across the EU, any regulatory initiatives, horizontal or sector-specific, should be aligned. In this regard, pragmatic and inclusive guidance should be provided by the EU legislator and the EU competent authorities to harmonise the various obligations of the obliged entities and promote a coherent interpretation. Although the AML Proposal is aiming to further articulate and align the interplay between GDPR and AML framework, considering the sensitivity of the processing operations and the particular characteristics of the highly regulated financial sector, without prejudice to the competences of AMLA, it appears that a joint guidance issued by EDPB, EDPS and EBA is more suitable.

As the European legislators contemplate upon the AIA and the AML Package, they should take into consideration the criticism of the proposals and the experience collected by the enforcement of AMLD and GDPR over the past year, and aim to harmonise or link the various obligations to avoid duplication and overburdening obliged entities. Notwithstanding, when it comes to AI-based AML/CFT systems, it should be noted that the unique characteristics of AI do not exclude the application of existing tools to help promote compliance for obliged entities. In any case, some guidance regarding outsourcing when AI-systems are used may be necessary, particularly to clarify the further processing activities carried by AI-providers and the accuracy of watchlists.

In any case, irrespective of the authority issuing guidance, any efficient policy initiative requires the support and collaboration of the AI and AML/CFT ecosystem. In this regard, it is important to carry an EU-wide mapping exercise identifying the different data processing operations followed by obliged entities, including when and which type of AI systems they deploy, to assess their suitability for the purposes of AML/CFT as well as whether they are proportionate and in line with the fundamental rights of privacy and data protection.

Lastly, complementing the effort of the AML Proposal to promote sharing of information amongst EU-based obliged entities and increasing robustness of identification and verification tools across the EU, data sharing through the EU common data spaces may further promote a data protection culture amongst obliged entities, while boosting efficiency of AML/CFT practices. This is also in line with the Proposal for a Data Governance Act [11], where one of the sectors identified in economy and finance.

References

1. Article 29 Data Protection Working Party: Opinion 14/2011 on data protection issues related to the prevention on money laundering and terrorist financing, adopted on 13 June 2011 (2011)
2. Article 29 Data Protection Working Party: Guidelines on Automated individual decision-making and Profiling for the purposes of Regulation 2016/679, adopted on 3 October 2017, as last revised and adopted on 6 February 2018 (2018)
3. Article 29 Data Protection Working Party: Guidelines on Data Protection Impact Assessment (DPIA) and determining whether processing is "likely to result in a high risk" for the purposes of Regulation 2016/679, adopted on 4 April 2017, as last revised and adopted on 4 October 2017 (2017)
4. Bertrand, A., Maxwell, W., Vamparys, X.: Are AI-based anti-money laundering (AML) systems compatible with european fundamental rights?. In: Telecom Paris Research Paper Series (2020). https://papers.ssrn.com/sol3/papers.cfm?abstract_id=3647420
5. Brewczynska, M.: Financial intelligence units: reflections on the applicable data protection legal framework. Comput. Law Secur. Rev. (2021). https://doi.org/10.1016/j.clsr.2021.105612
6. European Banking Authority: Final Report on EBA Guidelines on Outsourcing Arrangements (2019). https://www.eba.europa.eu/sites/default/documents/files/documents/10180/2551996/38c80601-f5d7-4855-8ba3-702423665479/EBA%20revised%20Guidelines%20on%20outsourcing%20arrangements.pdf?retry=1
7. European Banking Authority: Final Report on Guidelines on the characteristics of a Risk-based Supervision under Article 48(10) of Directive (EU) 2015/849 (2021). https://www.eba.europa.eu/sites/default/documents/files/document_library/Publications/Guidelines/2021/EBA-GL-2021-16%20GL%20on%20RBA%20to%20AML%20CFT/1025507/EBA%20Final%20Report%20on%20GL%20on%20RBA%20AML%20CFT.pdf
8. European Commission: Communication from the Commission on an Action Plan for a comprehensive Union policy on preventing money laundering and terrorist financing (2020/C 164/06) (2021)
9. European Commission: Proposal for a Directive of the European Parliament and of the Council on the mechanisms to be put in place by the Member States for the prevention of the use of the financial system for the purposes of money laundering or terrorist financing COM (2021) 423 (2021)
10. European Commission: Proposal for a Regulation of the European Parliament and of the Council Laying Down Harmonised Rules on Artificial Intelligence (Artificial Intelligence Act) and Amending Certain Union Legislative Acts, COM/2021/206 final (2021). https://eur-lex.europa.eu/legal-content/EN/TXT/?uri=CELEX%3A52021PC0206

11. European Commission: Proposal for a Regulation of the European Parliament and of the Council on European Data Governance (Data Governance Act) COM (2020) 767 final (2020). file:///C:/Users/IMK/Downloads/090166e5d6411f89.pdf
12. European Commission: Proposal for a Regulation of the European Parliament and of the Council on the prevention of the use of the financial system for the purposes of money laundering or terrorist financing COM (2021) 420 final (2021)
13. European Data Protection Board: Guidelines 06/2020 on the interplay of the Second Payment Services Directive and the GDPR, version 2.0, adopted, 15 October 2020 (2020). https://edpb.europa.eu/sites/default/files/files/file1/edpb_guidelines_202006_psd2_a fterpublicconsultation_en.pdf
14. Letter of Andrea Jelinek, Chair of the EDPB to Ms. Mairead McGuiness, European Commissioner for Financial services, financial stability and Capital Markets Union and Mr. Didier Reynders, European Commissioner for Justice, on 19 May 2021 (2021). https://edpb.europa. eu/system/files/2021-05/letter_to_ec_on_proposals_on_aml-cft_en.pdf
15. European Data Protection Board: Statement on the protection of personal data processed in relation with the prevention of money laundering and terrorist financing, adopted on 15 December 2020 (2020)
16. European Data Protection Supervisor: Opinion 12/2021 on the anti-money laundering and countering the financing of terrorism (AML/CFT) package of legislative proposals, 22 September 2021 (2021)
17. European Data Protection Supervisor: Opinion 5/2020 on the European Commission's action plan for a comprehensive Union policy on preventing money laundering and terrorism financing (2020). https://edps.europa.eu/sites/edp/files/publication/20-07-23_edps_aml_opi nion_en.pdf
18. Financial Action Task Force: International Standards on Combating Money Laundering and the Financing of Terrorism & Proliferation. (2012–2021). www.fatf-gafi.org/recommendati ons.html
19. Financial Action Task Force: Methodology for Assessing Technical Compliance with FATF Recommendations and the Effectiveness of AML/CFT Systems, adopted in February 2013, updated in November 2020 (2013). https://www.fatf-gafi.org/media/fatf/documents/method ology/FATF%20Methodology%2022%20Feb%202013.pdf
20. Koster, H.: Towards better implementation of the European Union's anti-money laundering and countering the financing of terrorism framework. J. Money Laundering Control 23(2), 379–386 (2020). https://doi.org/10.1108/JMLC-09-2019-0073
21. Maglieri, G., Comandé, G.: Why a right to legibility of automated decision-making exists in the general data protection regulation. Int. Data Priv. Law 7(3), 243 (2017). https://papers. ssrn.com/sol3/papers.cfm?abstract_id=3088976
22. Maxwell, W.: The GDPR and private sector measures to detect criminal activity. Revue des Affaires européennes - Law & European Affairs (2021). https://papers.ssrn.com/sol3/papers. cfm?abstract_id=3964066
23. Milaj, J., Kaiser, C.: Retention of data in the new anti-money laundering directive—'need to know' versus 'nice to know'. Int. Data Priv. Law 7(2), 115–125 (2017). https://doi.org/10. 1093/idpl/ipx002
24. Quintel, T.: Follow the Moneym if you can: possible solutions for enhanced FIU cooperation under improved data protection rules. Law Working Paper Series, Paper number 2019–001 (2019). https://papers.ssrn.com/sol3/papers.cfm?abstract_id=3318299
25. Wachter, S., Brent M., Floridi, L.: Why a right to explanation of automated decision-making does not exist in the general data protection regulation. Int. Data Priv. Law 7(3), 47 (2017). https://papers.ssrn.com/sol3/papers.cfm?abstract_id=2903469

Data Protection and Machine-Learning-Supported Decision-Making at the EU Border: ETIAS Profiling Under Scrutiny

Paulina Jo Pesch[1]([✉]), Diana Dimitrova[2,3], and Franziska Boehm[1]

[1] Karlsruhe Institute of Technology (KIT), 76131 Karlsruhe, Germany
paulina.pesch@kit.edu
[2] FIZ Karlsruhe - Leibniz Institute for Information Infrastructures, 76344
Eggenstein-Leopoldshafen, Germany
[3] Vrije Universiteit Brussel, LSTS Group, Brussels, Belgium

Abstract. ETIAS is an upcoming, largely automated IT system to identify risks posed by visa-exempt Third Country Nationals (TCNs) traveling to the Schengen area. It is expected to be operational by the end of 2022. The largely automated ETIAS risk assessments include the check of traveller data against not yet defined abstract risk indicators which might discriminate against certain groups of travellers. Moreover, there is evidence for the planned use of machine learning (ML) for risk assessments under the ETIAS framework. The risk assessments that could result in personal data being entered into terrorist watchlists or in a refusal of a travel authorisation have strong impacts especially on the fundamental right to data protection. The use of ML-trained models for such risk assessments raises concerns, since existing models lack transparency and, in some cases, have been found to be significantly biased. The paper discusses selected requirements under EU data protection law for ML-trained models, namely human oversight, information and access rights, accuracy, and supervision. The analysis considers provisions of the AI Act Proposal of the European Commission as the proposed regulation can provide guidance for the application of existing data protection requirements to AI.

Keywords: Machine learning · Artificial intelligence · Automated decisions · Data protection · EU border control

1 Introduction

At the EU border models trained with machine learning (ML) algorithms are already in use [40]. There is evidence for the use of such models also in ETIAS. ML-trained models promise to efficiently solve numerous problems based on huge amounts of data. They are particularly used for risk assessments [4, 49, 74]. However, the accountability of

A. Gryszczyńska et al. (Eds.): APF 2022, LNCS 13279, pp. 50–72, 2022.
https://doi.org/10.1007/978-3-031-07315-1_4

such data-driven models is still immature and creating models that can explain why they produce a certain output for a given input is an open research goal [67, 78]. In addition, some existing models have been found to be significantly biased [20, 72, 97]. This poses risks to data protection and other fundamental rights when feeding such models with personal data. Having said this, the use of ML in areas which can particularly affect fundamental rights, such as EU border control, is worrying.

This paper focuses on potential ML use cases in the European Travel and Information System (ETIAS) for traveller risk assessments. Against the background of the fundamental rights impacts of ETIAS, the paper discusses selected requirements of EU data protection law for ML trained models, namely human oversight, the rights to information and access to the decision-making logic of profiling measures, accuracy, and supervision.

The paper is structured as follows: Sect. 2 briefly introduces ETIAS, explaining the objectives and measures laid down in the ETIAS Regulation [81]. Section 3 outlines potential use cases for ML in ETIAS. Section 4 sums up fundamental rights impacts. Section 5 examines the application of selected EU data protection requirements to ML models. Section 6 draws a conclusion and addresses the remaining challenges.

2 The ETIAS System

ETIAS is an upcoming, largely automated IT system to identify security, irregular migration or high epidemic risks posed by visa-exempt Third Country Nationals (TCNs) traveling to the Schengen area, Art. 1 (1), rec. 2 ETIAS Regulation [81]. It is expected to be operational by the end of 2022 [47] and shall be developed by the European Agency for the operational management of large-scale IT-systems in the area of freedom, security and justice (eu-LISA), Art. 6 (1), also see Art. 73 (3) ETIAS Regulation [81]. The ETIAS Regulation anchors the requirement of a traveling authorisation that visa-exempt TCNs travelling to the Schengen area have to apply for prior to their trip or before expiry of an existing travel authorisation they hold, Art. 1 (1), 15 (1) ETIAS Regulation [81]. The travel authorisation is issued or refused based on a two-step risk assessment that takes into account the personal data to be provided by the applicants, Art. 17 ETIAS Regulation [81].

In the *first part of the risk assessment*, the ETIAS Central System *automatically* processes the application file to identify hits, Art. 20 (1) ETIAS Regulation [81]. The data are checked against a pre-determined list of EU information systems and Interpol data, Art. 12 and Art. 20 (2) ETIAS Regulation [81].[1] The data are checked, among others, against data in the Schengen Information System (SIS), e.g. to find out whether the applicant is subject to a refusal of entry and stay alert entered in SIS, and against Europol data, in the latter case without any further specification, Art. 20 (2) (a), (c), (d), (m), (j) ETIAS Regulation [81]. Furthermore, the ETIAS screening rules are applied, and

---

[1] Schengen Information System (SIS), Visa Information System (VIS), Entry-Exit System (EES), Eurodac, Europol data and Interpol SLTD and TDAWN.

the data are checked against the ETIAS watchlist, Art. 22 (3), 33, 34 ETIAS Regulation [81].[2]

The **ETIAS screening rules** are an 'algorithm enabling profiling' in the meaning of Art. 4 point 4 GDPR [79] and refer to the comparison of the data with specific risk indicators, Art. 33 (1) ETIAS Regulation [81]. The determination of risk indicators formally follows a two-step procedure: In a first step, the Commission defines and specifies risks related to security, illegal immigration or high epidemic risks based on statistical data and further information, Art. 33 (2–3) ETIAS Regulation [81]. The risks are extracted from various data, including statistics on abnormal rates of overstays or entry refusals for specific groups of travellers (e.g. generated in ETIAS or the Entry-Exit System). In a second step, based on the specified risks, the ETIAS Central Unit, a unit within the European Border and Coast Guard Agency (Frontex) (Art. 7 (1) ETIAS Regulation [81]), defines the risk indicators after consultation of the ETIAS Screening Board (Art. 9 ETIAS Regulation [81]), Art. 33 (4), (6) ETIAS Regulation [81]. The risk indicators shall consist of data including age range, sex, nationality, residence, education level, and occupation, Art. 33 (5) ETIAS Regulation [81]. In fact, there is no clear delineation between risks and indicators, as the risk specification is already based on data that imply certain risk indicators, for example statistical data on specific groups of travellers and risk indicators defined by the Member States.

The **ETIAS watchlist** contains data related to persons who are deemed to have committed or taken part in a terrorist or serious crime offence 'or persons regarding whom there are factual indications or reasonable grounds, based on an overall assessment of the person, to believe that they will commit a terrorist offence or other serious criminal offence', Art. 34 (1) ETIAS Regulation [81]. This wording is also typically used in EU law enforcement instruments such as Art. 18 Europol Regulation [80] or Art. 36 (3) (c) SIS Regulation [83]. Neither in the latter nor in the ETIAS Regulation it is clear which criteria apply, and which technologies are used to assess and determine that a person might commit a crime in future. Both Europol and Member States can enter data into the watchlist, Art. 34 (3) ETIAS Regulation [81].

If the automated processing produces no hit, the ETIAS Central System automatically issues a travel authorisation, Art. 21 (1) ETIAS Regulation [81]. Where the system reports one or more hits, in the *second part of the risk assessment*, the data are *manually processed*. The ETIAS Central Unit verifies the hit(s), Art. 22 ETIAS Regulation [81]. If the application data are found not to correspond to the risk indicators or data from the relevant databases or the watchlist, the ETIAS Central Unit issues the travel authorisation, Art. 22 (4) ETIAS Regulation [81]. Otherwise, or where there remain doubts concerning the identity of the applicant, the responsible ETIAS National Unit, a competent authority to be designated by each Member State (Art. 8 (1) ETIAS Regulation [81]), manually processes the application file, and then either issues or refuses a travel authorisation, Art. 22 (5), 25, 26 ETIAS Regulation [81].

---

[2] The ETIAS screening rules are planned to be used in future also when examining the risk of visa applicants (VIS Reg [84], Art. 9j), who will also be checked against the ETIAS watchlist (ibid., Art. 9a and 22b).

3 Machine Learning in ETIAS

While the ETIAS Regulation [81] foresees the partial automation of risk assessments and decisions based on these, as a technology-neutral legislative act, it does not specify the technological means. Looking at recent documents by eu-LISA and the Commission, there is evidence for the planned use of ML-trained models concerning the decision-making and risk assessments on TCN travellers.[3] Section 3.1 sums up ML fundamentals and characteristic issues. Section 3.2 illustrates potential use cases for ML-based risk assessments in ETIAS.

3.1 Machine Learning in a Nutshell

Machine learning (ML) is the most relevant field of artificial intelligence (AI). AI refers to intelligent machines while the concept of intelligence is not easy to define [66]. Broadly speaking, AI means machines that can learn, reason, and act for themselves [57]. ML refers to machines that recognise patterns in usually massive amounts of data. ML is especially used to train models for automated risk assessments [4, 49, 74]. An example is the software 'Correctional Offender Management Profiling for Alternative Sanctions' (COMPAS) that has been used by US courts: It is designed to assess the risks of persons failing to appear in court or recommitting a crime [71, 77], based, for example, on data on criminal history, age at first arrest, residential stability, employment status, and substance abuse [77], gathered through a questionnaire [1].

While ML-trained models promise to efficiently solve various problems and are already ubiquitous [cf. 76], many existing models have been found to discriminate against specific populations because of bias [20, 72, 97]. For example, COMPAS has been found to be twice as likely to falsely classify black defendants as future criminals compared to white defendants [1]. Bias in ML-trained models usually results from biased training data ('garbage in, garbage out') [50] and should be avoided in the first place by using non-biased training data, but the real world is biased. Developers might inadvertently collect and label[4] training data that confirm or strengthen their existing beliefs (*confirmation bias*), or select training data that systematically differ from the data the model is applied to when deployed (*selection bias*) [54]. Also, bias can be intentionally ingrained in models (see, for example, [75]). Hence, it is crucial to detect bias in ML-trained models. However, bias detection can be difficult, especially because the models do not provide explanations. It is crucial that models are evaluated with unbiased, sufficiently representative testing data [65].[5] Since data sets used for machine learning must be large, representative, and labelled, their preparation is very cost-intensive [61].

Existing ML-trained models are non-transparent but approaches for explainable AI (XAI) are discussed among experts [67, 78]. Current models referred to as XAI only show a certain degree of interpretability, though, while truly explainable AI is an unachieved research goal [25, 67, 78].

---

[3] See Sect. 3.2.

[4] The most prevalent approach to ML, supervised learning, refers to training models with labelled data, i.e. the training data consists of inputs and desired outputs [51].

[5] In this context see Art. 10 (3), Rec. 44 AI Act Proposal [28] that require data sets to be, among other things, sufficiently representative, accurate and complete.

Where ML-trained models are used for risk assessments, potentially built-in bias is not the only source of mistakes. No method for automated assessments, no matter whether ML is used or not and whether the model is biased or not, is 100 percent accurate. Any model produces errors, i.e. false positives and false negatives. Despite that, humans show a tendency to over-rely on the results of automated processing-procedures (*automation bias*) [52]. However, humans themselves make errors, too, and their error rates can be higher [91].

3.2 Potential Use of AI in ETIAS

While the ETIAS Regulation [81] clearly stipulates some degree of automation regarding the decision-making, neither the ETIAS Regulation, nor the respective delegated or implementing acts mention the use of ML specifically or artificial intelligence in general. However, eu-LISA, which shall develop the ETIAS Information System and ensure its technical management, in its report on 'Artificial Intelligence in the Operational Management of Large-scale IT systems' (hereinafter: eu-LISA AI report) [43] provides evidence for the intended use of ML-trained models for risk assessments in ETIAS.

In particular, the eu-LISA AI report includes a section on AI-enabled services in the context of new systems, mainly referring to ETIAS [43]. More specifically, 'an additional level of automation or analytics based on AI or machine learning could be introduced when dealing with any "suspicious" applications', 'support[ing] case officers responsible for evaluating applications with additional risk assessment based on the data stored in the relevant systems and the historical data on the [applicant]' [43]. Possible outcomes would be either a binary suggestion (issue or refuse a travel authorisation), or a risk grading [43]. The report states that some cases would require 'a more sophisticated system using one of the machine learning approaches' and names ML-trained models in credit risk analysis as an example [43]. By this, eu-LISA vaguely outlines an ML-trained model for risk assessments that is trained, tested, and used with diverse data from various sources. The 'data stored in the relevant systems and the historical data on the applicants include, but are not limited to, the risk indicators which the ETIAS screening rules are based on, and data from the ETIAS watchlist, as well as data from all databases[6] that are queried in the ETIAS risk assessments according to Art. 12, 20 (2) ETIAS Regulation [81], e.g. Europol databases and the SIS.

In addition to the eu-LISA AI report, the Commission's report on 'Opportunities and Challenges for the Use of Artificial Intelligence in Border Control, Migration and Security' (hereinafter: Commission AI report) [27] also explicitly mentions individual risk assessments in cases of hits under ETIAS as a use case for ML.

It is noteworthy that neither of the two reports substantially addresses risks or fundamental rights implications of ML-trained risk assessment models. The Commission AI report mentions the risk of inaccurate results but only presents a 'human in the loop to [...] review outputs' as a solution, without addressing the issue of automation bias (the human tendency to over-rely on automation)[7] [27]. In the context of ETIAS, it does

---

[6] Schengen Information System (SIS), Visa Information System (VIS), Entry-Exit System (EES), Eurodac, Europol data and Interpol SLTD and TDAWN.

[7] See Sect. 2.

not refer to the risks of misuse and bias, while mentioning these in the context of other AI use cases.[8] The eu-LISA AI report states errors and biases could be 'reduced, if not completely avoided' by 'testing [and training] AI solutions on representative data sets' without further explanation [43]. In the context of ETIAS, the eu-LISA report vaguely addresses 'ethical implications', stating a human should be involved without mentioning automation bias or how concretely human involvement could mitigate possible ethical or legal infringements [43].

There are even more potential use cases for risk assessments using ML-trained models in the context of ETIAS than the reports mention. The risk assessments, based on which data related to persons likely to commit a terrorist offence or other serious criminal offence in the future is entered into the ETIAS watchlist (Art. 34 ETIAS Regulation [81]), could rely on ML-trained models. The ETIAS Regulation does not specify how Europol and the Member States determine whose personal data to enter in the ETIAS watchlist. It merely states that it shall be established based on information related to terrorist offences or other serious criminal offences (Art. 34 (2) ETIAS Regulation [81]), but not how and with what measures this information is obtained and finally entered.

Also, some of the data in the databases that the application files are automatically compared against could be the result of risk assessments using ML-trained models, although this is not explicitly stated anywhere. In particular, the SIS alerts that ETIAS application data are checked against according to Art. 20 (2) (c) ETIAS Regulation [81], comprise data based on risk assessments: Under the SIS Regulation, alerts can be entered for persons who, based on an overall assessment, are believed to commit certain offences in future Art. 36 (3) (c) [83].[9] Furthermore, the Europol data that Art. 20 (2) (j) ETIAS regulation [81] generally refers to,[10] also include data on possible future perpetrators, Art. 18 (2) (a) (ii) Europol Regulation [80], whose risk profiles might be generated with ML-trained models,[11] too.

Another potential use case for ML in ETIAS is the use of ML-trained models in the risk indicator specification process. Namely, ML-trained models could be used for the determination of risks based on statistics (Art. Art. 33 (2) ETIAS Regulation [81]).

4   Interferences with Fundamental Rights

In particular two measures, namely the placing on the ETIAS watchlist and the above-discussed ETIAS risk assessment, both can lead to the refusal to grant a travel authorisation by an officer at an ETIAS National Unit. Both measures may take place with

---

[8] For example, the Commission AI report refers to misuse and bias in the context of EU policy making and enforcement process [27].

[9] The provision refers to the offences referred to in Art. 2 (1) and 2 (2) of the Framework decision 2002/584/JHA [13].

[10] '[D]ata recorded in Europol data'.

[11] Europol has used Palantir Gotham for the operational analysis of counter terrorism related data according to *the Commission's* answer to a parliamentary question [41]. The software is promoted as 'AI-ready' [73]. Some national law enforcement agencies use AI tools already, see, for example, [37].

the help of ML. This section tries to narrow down which fundamental rights could be interfered with, and which should be subject to a more detailed observation later.

From both Courts, the European Court of Human Rights (ECtHR) and the Court of Justice of the European Union (CJEU), it is clear that to fulfil the necessity and proportionality requirements (Art. 52 (1) CFREU [11] and Art. 8 (2) ECHR [12]), which are two of the requirements for justifying the interference with fundamental rights, the measures need to be accompanied in particular by *adequate safeguards* when automated data processing and profiling is involved [15, 19, 29, 30]. The safeguards established in these judgments concern in particular human involvement, transparency, accuracy, and effective supervision. Whether the current framework provides for such safeguards will be discussed in Sect. 5. This section gives a brief overview of the most important rights being interfered with, to be then able to start a more detailed discussion on the safeguards that ML-trained models for risk assessments under ETIAS call for in the subsequent analysis.

First, it should be noted that a travel authorisation refusal can have a huge impact on the applicants' *private, family and professional lives* (Art. 7 CFREU [11] and Art. 8 ECHR [12]) which is a broad notion [34]. It might prevent foreigners, for example, from seeking specialised medical care [32][12], from closing a business deal[13] or simply from seeing family members or friends. In addition, the data analysis under ETIAS could reveal 'very specific information' about people's private lives, at least as concerns their travel (see by analogy [19]). In that context, risk profiling algorithms which result in or lead to incorrect presumptions of risk in individual cases and serve as a basis for refusal decisions, could interfere with the right to private life.

Second, the use of automated data processing – especially with the help of ML [19][14] – in ETIAS, and the transmission of data from Europol and the Member States onto the ETIAS watchlist [35] interfere intensely with the fundamental *right to data protection* which is laid down in Art. 8 CFREU [11] and can touch upon the provisions of Art. 8 (2) CFREU on fair processing. Where such a processing is, for instance, biased or not accurate, produces discriminatory results [53] or is not transparent [42], data protection and non-discrimination rights are interfered with [19, 18], Art. 8, 20 CFREU [11]. Discriminatory data processing and entry refusals can especially occur because of discriminatory risk indicators or inaccurate data in the relevant databases [93] or biased ML-trained models for risk assessments (see Sect. 5.4).

Furthermore, when supported by ML-trained models, decisions to refuse a travel authorisation could lack transparency. More concretely, this would be the case where an applicant is not provided with information about how and why they were considered a threat, or a possible threat (i.e. likely to commit a crime in future) as a result of the risk assessment, why they are listed in the ETIAS watchlist, or why an officer at the ETIAS National Unit concluded during the manual verification that an applicant indeed poses a risk and should be refused an authorisation. It might be difficult to understand, both for

[12] On the impossibility to travel for medical purposes due to a UN blacklist.
[13] According to the ECtHR, professional relations can be considered private life under Art. 8 ECHR [31] (on an impossibility to travel for medical and business purposes due to an entry ban in the SIS).
[14] See para 126 and the case-law cited there.

the officers and the concerned individuals, what criteria exactly produced the hit, how they should be interpreted and possibly challenged. Where a risk assessment is based on risk indicators defined by the Commission and Frontex, the officers from the National Units are hardly able to assess these factors' actual significance for the individual case. Refusal decisions that lack transparency might also lead to restrictions in the exercise of the rights of access and rectification, which also form part of the right to data protection, Art. 8 (2) CFREU [11]. If applicants do not understand how such conclusions were reached, the process remains non-transparent, and they cannot challenge the legality of the processing as well as the decisions of the system and the officers [39].

Third, applicants not being able to challenge a suspected data protection breach because of insufficient access or missing information may lead to an interference with the *right to effective remedies* laid down in Art. 47 CFREU [11] and Art. 13 ECHR [12, 6, 14][15]. The right to effective remedies includes not only the right to challenge the refusal to issue a travel authorisation, but also the right to challenge the information or data on which the refusal decision was based [7]. Similar to surveillance cases, in which, for example, access to secret service files is always subject to a difficult weighing of interests [33], it appears to be also very hard for a concerned ETIAS applicant to prove that the criteria leading to a travel refusal are based on wrong information concerning them or that they are discriminatory or irrelevant, in particular if the decision leading to the refusal was taken with the help of AI.

There are many details to be clarified with regard to important fundamental rights such as private and family life and the right to effective remedies. However, the finding that entries in the ETIAS watchlist and the ETIAS risk assessments intensely interfere with the right to data protection calls for a further analysis of the ETIAS measures under data protection law. The potential consequences of a refusal of the travel authorisation and impacts on other fundamental rights make strong safeguards necessary.

5   ML-Trained Models in ETIAS Under EU Data Protection Law

Under EU data protection law (see Sect. 5.1 on the applicable provisions), the use of ML-trained models for risk assessment to support decisions especially raises questions regarding automated decision-making and human oversight (Sect. 5.2), information and access rights (Sect. 5.3), as well as accuracy (Sect. 5.4). Since the fundamental rights impacts summed up in Sect. 4 make strong safeguards necessary, effective and independent supervision is crucial (Sect. 5.5).

5.1   Applicable EU Data Protection Provisions

The ETIAS Regulation itself lays down provisions concerning the protection of data only to a limited extent and stipulates that Regulation (EU) 2018/1725 [82] (hereinafter: EUDPR), the General Data Protection Regulation (hereinafter: GDPR) [79], and the Law Enforcement Directive (hereinafter: LED) [24] apply to the processing of personal

---

[15] On Art. 47 CFREU [11].

data under the ETIAS Regulation, Art. 56 (1^{16}–3) ETIAS Regulation [81]. The data protection provisions of the Europol Regulation apply to the personal data processing by Europol [80], Art. 56 (4) ETIAS Regulation [81].

Specifically, the EUDPR [82] applies to the personal data processing by Frontex, including the processing activities of the ETIAS Central Unit, as well as to the personal data processing by eu-LISA, (cf. Art. 26 ff. EUDPR [82]). The GDPR [79] applies to the personal data processing by the ETIAS National Units, unless the data are processed for the purposes of the prevention, detection or investigation of terrorist offences or of other serious offences, which falls under the scope of the LED [24], Art. 56 (2) ETIAS Regulation [81].

In practice, the participation of different EU and national authorities in the definition of the risk indicators, entering data in the relevant databases, and the risk assessment, as well as the mix of law enforcement and non-law enforcement purposes of the risk assessment, complicate the determination of the provisions applicable to a specific data processing (e.g. a manual risk assessment, based on risk indicators or an entry in the watchlist). This in turn could pose a problem for the harmonised application and enforcement of the data protection safeguards in practice.[17]

Furthermore, the European Commission proposed a Regulation laying down harmonised rules on artificial intelligence (hereinafter: AI Act Proposal) that, among other objectives, aims to ensure AI systems' compliance with fundamental rights, especially the respect for private life and the protection of personal data, and shall complement European data protection law [28] (see a critical overview in [94]). Albeit the AI Act, as proposed by the Commission, is unlikely to apply to ML-trained models used for ETIAS risk assessments as it statutes an exemption for systems already in use,[18] its specifications of requirements laid down in the existing data protection law can provide guidance for the application of these requirements to AI systems. Furthermore, the exemption for systems already in use, that has been criticised by the European Data Protection Board (EDPB) and the European Data Protection Supervisor (EDPS) [26], could be omitted in the final version of the AI Act. Therefore, the further analysis refers to the AI Act Proposal's specifications on the requirements of human oversight and accuracy for AI

---

[16] The provision refers to the predecessor Regulation (EC) No 45/2001 that has been replaced by the EUDPR [82].

[17] For information and access rights see Sect. 5.3 with fn. 28, 31.

[18] Specifically, the AI Act Proposal [28] statutes an exemption for AI systems which are components of the large-scale IT systems established by the legal acts listed in Annex IX that have been placed on the market or put into service before 12 months after the date of application of the proposed AI Act, Art. 83 (1). The AI Act shall apply after 24 months following its entry into force, Art. 85 (2). Annex IX lists union legislations on large-scale IT systems in the area of freedom, security and justice, particularly the regulations concerning ETIAS (Nr. 5) that is expected to be operational by end of 2022 and hence is highly likely to fall under the exemption according to the AI Act Proposal [28]. However, the AI Act Proposal [28] stipulates that the requirements of the proposed regulation shall be taken into account in the evaluation of the exempted AI systems, Art. 83 (1). ETIAS will be evaluated three years after the start of operations and every four years thereafter, Art. 92 (5) ETIAS Regulation [81].

systems such as ML-trained models (Art. 3 (1), Annex I (a) AI Act Proposal [28])[19] that pose high risks[20] to fundamental rights.[21]

5.2 Human Oversight

Generally, under EU data protection law, data subjects shall not be subject to decisions based solely on automated processing, which produce legal effects[22] concerning them or similarly significantly affect them Art. 24 EUDPR [82], Art. 22, rec. 71 GDPR [79], Art. 11, LED [24]. Under the ETIAS Regulation, in particular, the refusal of a travel authorisation is a decision that produces legal effects concerning applicants, cf. [2[23]]. Automated processing refers to any operation or set of operations which is performed on personal data or on sets of personal data in an automated manner, Art. 3 (3) EUDPR [82], Art. 4 (2) GDPR [79], Art. 3 (2), LED [24]. The automated checks in the ETIAS risk assessment (i.e. data base query, the application of the ETIAS screening rules and the check against the ETIAS watchlist), as well as the use of ML-trained models to support decisions, all fall under the scope of that broad definition. Thus, the ETIAS National Units must not refuse a travel authorisation solely based on the outcome of the automated risk assessment by an ML-trained model.

Drawing the line between automated-decision-making and decisions that are merely supported by automated processing is crucial [2]. Solely automated decision-making refers to decisions without human involvement [2]. For a decision to be not solely based on automated processing, human oversight must be meaningful instead of a mere formality [2]. That not only requires the competence of the human decision-maker to change the decision, but also a critical assessment of the decision that the result of the automated processing suggests [2]. To do so, the human decision-maker needs to take into account all the relevant aspects of an individual case (cf. [85][24]).

Formally, the ETIAS Regulation provides for human involvement in decisions to refuse a travel authorisation. Where the automated processing produces a hit, the ETIAS Central Unit verifies this hit, and then forwards the application file to the responsible ETIAS National Unit to manually process the file and to decide whether to issue or refuse a travel authorisation, Art. 22 (1), (5), Art. 26 ETIAS Regulation [81].

It is hard to determine which information human decision-makers need to critically assess hits. For any probabilistic measures and measures relying on assumptions, such

---

[19] Cf. AI Act Proposal [28], Art. 3 (1), Annex I (a).

[20] AI Act Proposal [28], p. 7. The proposal particularly classifies AI systems intended to be used for assessing risks posed by persons who intend to enter into the territory of a Member State (e.g. further ETIAS risk assessments in case of a hit), and AI systems intended to be used for making individual risk assessments regarding the risk of future criminal offences (e.g. upstream risk assessments which SIS or Europol entries are based on) as high-risk, Art. 6 (2), annex III Nr.6 (a), III Nr.7 (b) AI Act Proposal [28].

[21] See Sects. 5.2 and 5.4.

[22] The LED provision explicitly covers 'adverse' legal effects only, Art. 11 (1) LED [24].

[23] The Art. 29 Working Party, WP251rev.01, p. 21 gives the 'refused admission to a country' as an example for such a decision.

[24] In the context of American prosecution procedure law ('totality-of-the-circumstances-analysis').

as risk assessments, human decision-makers must be aware of automation-bias,[25] the human tendency to over-rely on automation [48]. In order to avoid automation bias and really challenge the system's and ML-trained model's output, human decision-makers should have a sufficient understanding of the functioning and limitations of the automated processing, especially of the accuracy of its results [48]. This corresponds to the AI Act's specifications concerning human oversight [28]:[26] Art. 14 (1) stipulates high-risk AI systems must allow for effective oversight. Especially, decision-makers shall be enabled to fully understand the capacities and limitations of the system (Art. 14 (4) (a)), to remain aware of automation bias (Art. 14 (4) (b)), and to correctly interpret the system's output (Art. 14 (4) (c)). The provision is complemented by Art. 13 (1) that requires sufficient transparency of the system's operation to users to enable them to interpret its output (Art. 13 (1)). Furthermore, users must be provided with instructions for use that include concise, complete, correct and clear information that is relevant, accessible and comprehensible to users (Art. 13 (2)), with information on (output) accuracy and the relevant accuracy metrics (Art. 13 (3) (b) (ii), Art. 13 (3) (d)).

Trainings, instructions, and warnings implemented in the tools used can raise general awareness of automation-bias. However, it remains unclear how the tools for risk assessments with ML-trained models need to be designed and which exact information human decision-makers must be provided with to ensure effective oversight.

Where ML-trained models are used, human decision-makers might be unable to sufficiently check the results of automated risk assessments because ML-trained models do not deliver explanations. However, it is questionable whether explanations facilitate human oversight. Legally, human decision-makers need to assess the case, not the model or its outputs. In fact, they do not require an ML-trained models' explanation for finding an explanation for their decision. Furthermore, empirical studies have shown that human oversight does not necessarily benefit from explanations of automated systems' results [56]. Interpretable models that provide for transparency and present users with more features might, against their intentions, impede detecting and correcting for mistakes due to information overload [76]. Also, explanations can reinforce automation bias, and make it less likely that human decision-makers deviate from inaccurate results [55, 63, 76]. Empirical studies specifically examining impacts of the level of interpretability of automated ETIAS risk assessment results on the oversight by ETIAS officers seem desirable before ML-trained models are implemented.

In terms of tool design, the level of granularity of automated risk assessment results might impact human oversight. The eu-LISA AI report states that the output of a risk assessment based on ML-trained models could be either a binary suggestion or a risk grading [43]. A binary suggestion would consist in a recommendation either to refuse or to issue a travel authorisation without any differentiation. This could either trigger scrutiny or create a wrong impression of certainty. It is necessary to examine in behavioural studies how much differentiation is desirable to facilitate critical assessments of ML-trained models' recommendations (cf. [76]).

---

[25] See Sect. 3.1.
[26] See Sect. 5.1 on the applicability.

Even with the best qualification (in the context of the AI Act Proposal see [26]) and tools, it is fundamentally questionable that meaningful human oversight over tools is feasible at all [56]. The less humans responsible for overseeing models are able to provide for accuracy and non-discrimination, cf. [55], the more important it is that the models themselves are sufficiently accurate and non-discriminatory.[27]

As a side note, insufficient human oversight over ML-trained models is not the only concern when it comes to the manual assessment of ETIAS applications. As much as the officers from the ETIAS National Units could over-rely on automation, they might over-rely on data that other organisations, i.e. other Member States' National Units or Europol, have entered in the relevant databases. For such cases, Art. 28 f. ETIAS Regulation [81] stipulates the consultation of the respective organisation. However, there is a risk of misinterpretations of information provided, for example because of different understandings of legal terms (cf. [62]). Also, consulting a Member State or Europol in accordance with Art. 28 f. ETIAS Regulation [81] does not prevent decisions based on unlawfully gathered data, such as the massive amounts of data that Europol has stored without data subject categorisation and been ordered to delete by the European Data Protection Supervisor (EDPS) [38, 46] (also see [90]).

5.3 The Rights of Information and Access to the Decision-Making Logic

Apart from human oversight, the non-transparency of ML-trained technologies could impair data subjects' information and access rights. To ensure transparency of the data processing for the concerned individuals, EU data protection law grants data subjects both a right to information and a right to access to their personal data. What is questionable is how much information on ML-trained models and the results of the processing is required.

The provisions on both rights under the GDPR and the EUDPR, the right to information and the right to access, require the controller to inform data subjects 'if automated decision-making, including profiling' takes place, and to provide data subjects 'at least in those cases' with 'meaningful information about the logic involved, as well as the significance and the envisaged consequences of such processing for the data subject', Art. 15 (2) (f) EUDPR [82], Art. 15 (1) (h) GDPR [79].[28] The involved logic refers to the relevant factors taken into account and their weight [2].

It is not clear whether this requirement applies to fully automated decisions only or also to profiling if it just supports decisions. Under the ETIAS Regulation human involvement is required, even though there remain doubts about the practical implementation.[29] In any case, the risk assessments under ETIAS are performed by way of profiling that is defined as 'any automated processing of personal data consisting of the use of personal data to evaluate certain personal aspects relating to a natural person',

---

[27] On accuracy and non-discrimination see Sect. 5.4.

[28] No such explicit requirement exists under the LED, which demonstrates that the level of transparency provided for under the LED is lower as compared to the GDPR. This inconsistency could pose a problem where the determination of the applicable provisions is unclear (see Sect. 5.1).

[29] See Sect. 5.2.

Art. 3 (5) EUDPR [82], Art. 4 (4) GDPR [79], Art. 3 (4) LED [24]. Automated individual risk assessments which result in entries into the watchlist, the SIS, or Europol databases, as well as automated risk assessments supporting decisions to refuse travel authorisations fall under this definition. The ETIAS screening rules are even explicitly defined as an algorithm enabling profiling, Art. 33 (1) ETIAS Regulation [81].

The phrasing 'including profiling' implies that the provision applies to automated decisions, whether based on profiling or not, but not to mere profiling if it does not result in an automated decision [95, cf. 8]. However, the phrasing '*at least* in *those* cases' argues for a broader scope of the requirement to reveal the involved logic. By stating that 'at least' in cases of automated decision-making ('those cases') revealing the logic involved is necessary, the provision implies that in some cases of profiling (these cases) the same is required (cf. [3, 16]). For ETIAS risk assessments, their fundamental rights impact[30] argues for providing applicants with information on the involved logic being required. This is because the transparency obligations especially safeguard the rights of concerned individuals and shall enable them to efficiently exercise their rights. However, there remains legal uncertainty. The ETIAS organisations could argue that there is no need for revealing the logic of profiling models because the final decision is made by a human who independently examines the case decision [cf. 95]. But this argument ignores the potential influence of the ML-trained model to the decision.

For decisions based on profiling, whether automated or not, the right to access comprises a right to obtain an explanation of the specific decision reached after a profiling assessment, see Rec. 71 GDPR [79].[31] The exact content of the right to explanation, however, is unclear [2, 9, 10, 64, 68–70]. The purpose of the transparency requirements is key. They seek to improve the knowledge balance between controller and data subject [58], to enable a compliance assessment and to challenge the conclusions of the profiling technologies and of the responsible authorities [2, 86]. For risk assessments under ETIAS this means that applicants must receive enough information to understand why and based on which factors their data have been entered in the ETIAS watchlist or being refused a travel authorisation. To enable applicants to challenge a potential refusal of a travel authorisation and to check the compliance of the processing of their data with data protection law, it is necessary to provide them with diverse information: Applicants must know whether and, if so, why and by whom they have been placed on the ETIAS watchlist. They must know whether the comparison of their application data against the screening rules has led to a hit, and which criteria and reasoning the hit is based on. And they must be informed about the manual risk assessment. Questionable is how much information about the automated risk assessment models that are used to support the final decision-making is required. The AI Act Proposal does not clarify this for high-risk AI systems, as it does not specify data subjects' rights [28]. For applicants to challenge a decision supported by an ML-trained model, also in the light of the human oversight requirement,[32] they need to know which data are fed into the model and the result of the processing.

---

[30] See Sect. 4.

[31] This requirement is not explicitly anchored in the LED [24].

[32] See Sect. 5.2.

In order to enable applicants to challenge a refusal decision they need to be informed about the involved authorities, i.e. whether the opinion of another Member State or Europol played a role and which this other authority issued such an opinion [17][33]. For example, if the refusal followed a hit against the ETIAS watchlist, as entered by Europol, individuals might want to challenge their inclusion into the watchlist by Europol. In that case, they need to know about their inclusion into the watchlist and that it was Europol which entered them. Otherwise, if the alert is not challenged and deleted, Member States might be tempted to accept that the applicant poses a threat just by the mere fact that they are present in the watchlist or because Europol has stated so in their opinion sent to the Member State, which might remain unchallenged (see by analogy [17]).

5.4 Data and Profiling Model Accuracy

In the context of decisions supported by automated means accuracy is key – and it concerns two aspects, the accuracy of presented results and the accuracy of the model itself. Where ML-trained models are used in ETIAS to support the manual check of applications that produced a hit, or before entering data in the watchlist, the models' risk assessment results must be sufficiently accurate.

EU data protection law imposes data accuracy requirements. It particularly requires data controllers to keep personal data accurate, Art. 4 (1) (d) EUDPR [82], Art. 5 (1) (d) GDPR [79], Art. 4 (1) (d) LED [24]. While for factual data, such as names, addresses or criminal records, it is easier to draw a line between accurate and inaccurate data, it is questionable what the accuracy requirement means for probabilistic results and estimations, such as the risk assessments under ETIAS. A minimum requirement for such data is the meta-information that their character as probabilistic or estimated is apparent from the data because otherwise they falsely imply to reflect facts [48].

In addition, the profiling criteria must lead to sufficiently accurate results so that they produce correct decisions. The use of ML-trained models that produce inaccurate results is not justifiable, because this could be seen as a breach of the data protection principles, e.g. the purpose limitation principle, Art. 4 (1) (c) EUDPR [82], Art. 5 (1) (c) GDPR [79], Art. 4 (1) (c) LED [24]. Data protection law only allows for the processing of data necessary for a certain purpose. Processing applicants' data with ML-trained models with a very low accuracy would not fulfil the purposes of ETIAS, because it could result in people who actually do not pose a risk to be refused travel authorisations, and in people who do pose a risk to receive a travel authorisation, defeating the purposes for which the personal data are processed (cf. [23, 48]). For risk assessments, in addition to the correct input data, also a certain minimum degree of reliability of the underlying models and applied criteria is necessary to arrive at reasonable risk assessment results [18, 19].

For the ETIAS watchlist, Art. 35 ETIAS Regulation [81] explicitly addresses accuracy: It requires (1) assessing the necessity for entering a name on the list before a name is entered and (2) regular reviews of the accuracy of the data on the list and the continued necessity to store the said data on the list. This applies to the data entered into the ETIAS

---

[33] In the context of visa decisions.

watchlist based on risk assessments. The AI Act Proposal [28][34] explicitly requires high-risk AI systems to achieve, in the light of their intended purpose, an appropriate level of accuracy that shall be determined based on metrics, Art. 15 (1–2).

In the context of accuracy, it is also important that the models and criteria must be non-discriminatory in the legal sense[35] [19]. This especially concerns the risk indicators that application data are checked against in the automated screening and that are also relevant to the further risk assessment where they have led to a hit (Art. 20 (5), 26 (5) ETIAS Regulation [81]). Art. 33 (5) sentence 2 ETIAS Regulation [81] prohibits risk indicators that are based on information revealing a person's colour, race, ethnic or social origin, genetic features, language, political or any other opinion, religion or philosophical belief, trade union membership, membership of a national minority, property, birth, disability or sexual orientation'. This requirement alone cannot sufficiently prevent discrimination, since risk indicators may indicate the prohibited information [93], just as the software COMPAS discriminated against black people without processing data on race [1]. Accordingly, ML-trained models for risk assessments in ETIAS will have to be checked carefully for hidden bias. Art. 10 AI Act Proposal [28] requires training, validation and testing data sets to meet quality criteria that particularly comprise examination in view of possible biases.

The accuracy and non-discrimination of ML-trained risk assessment models in ETIAS depends on the selection and preparation of sufficient training data on the one hand and thorough testing with adequate testing data on the other hand.[36] Gathering sufficient training and testing data is a challenge, since it is crucial to achieve accuracy for the real application data the ETIAS risk assessments are performed on, rather than 'overfit' the models to historical training and testing data, which do not necessarily reflect the changes in the underlying problems which a profiling model tries to solve [21, 96]. However, in practice, it is questionable whether authorities that are responsible for the development of ML-trained models can ensure and demonstrate sufficient accuracy, since outsourcing of the development is likely. To give an example in the EU Border Control context, eu-LISA has outsourced the development of the Shared Biometric Matching System (sBMS) [44], that comprises a deep-learning-trained tool [45], to Sopra Steria and IDEMIA [89], two companies engaged in the development of AI solutions [60, 88]. This can result in insufficient insight into the training of the models where the contractors keep training sets secret. One incentive for that is the high cost required for preparing training data sets for ML [61]. Furthermore, compliance with data protection law can be an issue: Where real-world personal data is required for the development of a model, the processing may only take place for a specific purpose based on a legal basis, Art. 6 (1) GDPR [79], Art. 5 (1) EUDPR [82], Art. 8 LED [24]. Where eu-LISA or National Units initiate the development of ML-trained risk assessment models but are not involved in the training, they need to ensure accuracy and non-discrimination by sufficient testing of models. However, it is questionable how they prepare sufficiently big and data protection compliant testing data sets. Synthetic data sets might solve data protection issues

[34] On the applicability of the AI Act Proposal [28] see Sect. 5.1.

[35] From a statistical point of view, discrimination is the objective of risk assessments. See, for example, on the discriminatory power of credit scorings [5].

[36] See Sect. 3.1.

[59] but are not necessarily sufficient to evaluate models for real-world use in ETIAS. Where real-world data are necessary sufficient testing might also require measures to avoid inadvertently using data that have been part of the training data set already.

For the accuracy of ML-trained models used in ETIAS it will also be crucial which minimum level of accuracy the authorities evaluating and applying them will require and how the accuracy is demonstrated. When assessing concrete models, potential trade-offs between accuracy and performance must be considered (cf. [87]). In the context of accuracy of predictive models, it is noteworthy that 100% accuracy might not only be impossible but also not desirable as, paradoxically, models with a given accuracy may produce better predictions than models with a higher accuracy [92]. In any case, models for which the accuracy is not determinable, must not be used. It is especially questionable for models assessing the risk of future terrorist offenses whether their level of accuracy can be determined.

5.5 Supervision and Enforcement

Against the background of the fundamental rights impacts of ETIAS risk assessments and data protection issues posed by ML-trained models effective and independent supervision and enforcement of the applicable requirements are crucial (cf. Art. 8 (3) CFREU [11]).

The data processing in the context of ETIAS is subject to supervision by multiple supervisory authorities. While the ETIAS National Units will be supervised by the data protection authorities (DPAs) in the Member States (Art. 66 (1) and (3) ETIAS Regulation [81]), the EDPS supervises Frontex, eu-LISA and Europol (Art. 67 ETIAS Regulation [81]). The ETIAS Regulation [81] stipulates a coordinated supervision and cooperation between the supervisory authorities (Art. 68 (1)) and requires them to meet at least twice a year (Art. 68 (3)). This coordinated supervision is organised by the EDPB and is anchored also in Art. 62 EUDPR [82] (see [36]).

On the one hand, coordinated supervision has the advantage that it allows for finding common solutions to issues that fall within the responsibility of more than one supervisory authority. On the other hand, it poses a risk to the supervisory authorities' independence in exercising their regulatory function. For example, since the Member State authorities, Europol, the Commission, and Frontex influence the definition and evaluation of the screening rules (Art. 33), it might not be immediately clear which supervisory authority bears the supervisory responsibility for ETIAS screenings and results, e.g. in cases of complaints by affected applicants. Also, it might be difficult to delineate responsibilities where a National Unit's decision to refuse a travel authorisation is Member State and Europol effectively jointly reach a refusal decision is based on Europol data only [22]. To ensure effective and independent supervision, the functioning of the coordinated supervision of ETIAS and other border control systems such as SIS (c.f. Art. 71 SIS Regulation [83]) or VIS (cf. Art. 43 VIS Regulation [84]) should be evaluated.

The development and use of ML-trained risk assessment models further complicates supervision, especially where the development of a model is (partially) outsourced and private companies are involved. In any case, outsourcing to private companies must not enable eu-LISA or the National Units to circumvent data protection law, especially the requirement of a legal basis for processing personal data for training models.

6   Conclusion and Future Work

The use of ML-trained models for ETIAS risk assessments, as envisaged by eu-LISA and the Commission, and refusals of travel authorisation based on such tools can have impacts on fundamental rights that call for strong safeguards. EU data protection law especially requires meaningful human oversight, information and access rights, and sufficient accuracy, as well as the effective supervision and enforcement of these requirements.

For ML-trained risk assessment models in ETIAS there remain many uncertainties and concerns. Any tool used should facilitate human oversight by design. Based on existing empirical research, however it is not yet clear, if, and if so, how this is possible. Officers at the National Units might not only blindly follow a tool's risk assessment due to automation-bias but, on top of that, insufficiently check data from other Member States or Europol, or overstate potentially discriminatory risk indicators defined by the Commission and Frontex. To enable applicants to challenge decisions to refuse travel authorisations, according to the provisions concerning information and access rights, the National Units need to give them sufficient information also regarding the risk assessments and authorities involved. Automated risk assessment models may only be used to support decisions if they reach sufficient accuracy levels and follow the non-discrimination principle. However, it still must be clarified which level of accuracy is required and desirable and whether accuracy can be measured for all risks that are assessed in ETIAS. Since the development of tools is likely to be outsourced to private companies that presumably do not disclose training data sets, evaluating tools with sufficient testing data is crucial but gathering and preparing data sets is cost-intensive and must comply with data protection requirements. The data processing in ETIAS, and probably also the development of ML-trained risk assessment models are subject to supervision by multiple supervisory authorities. Effective supervision and co-ordination of yet independent supervisory authorities are crucial.

Answers to the open questions and best practices can only be found in an interdisciplinary discourse bringing legal requirements, technical possibilities, and behavioural studies together. Against the background of the fundamental rights impacts of travel refusals under ETIAS or entries into the ETIAS watchlist, it is disconcerting that deploying ML-trained models for the underlying risk assessments is envisaged before the open questions have been further addressed.

Acknowledgements. The authors would like to thank Tobias Kupek, Rainer Böhme and our anonymous reviewers for valuable remarks.

Franziska Boehm and Paulina Jo Pesch participate in the project INDIGO (Information in the EU's Digitalized Governance). The project is financially supported by the NORFACE Joint Research Programme on Democratic Governance in a Turbulent Age and co-funded by AEI, AKA, DFG and FNR, and the European Commission through Horizon 2020 under grant agreement No. 822166.

This project has received funding from the European Union's Horizon 2020 research and innovation programme under grant agreement No 822166.

NORFACE
NETWORK

References

1. Angwin, J., Larson, J., Mattu, S., Kirchner, L.: Machine Bias. There's software used across the country to predict future criminals. And it's biased against blacks. ProPublica (2016). https://www.propublica.org/article/machine-bias-risk-assessments-in-criminal-sentencing. Accessed 04 Apr 2022
2. Article 29 Working Party: Guidelines on Automated individual decision-making and Profiling for the purposes of Regulation 2016/679, 17/EN WP251rev.01 (2018)
3. Bäcker, in: Kühling, J., Buchner, B.: Datenschutz-Grundverordnung, Bundesdatenschutzgesetz: DS-GVO/BDSG, 3rd edn, C.H. Beck (2020). Art. 13
4. Berk, R.: Criminal Justice Forecasts of Risks – A Machine Learning Approach. Springer, Berlin (2012). https://doi.org/10.1007/978-1-4614-3085-8
5. Blöchlinger, A., Leippold, M.: Economic benefit of powerful credit scoring. J. Bank. Finance **30**, 851–873 (2006)
6. Brkan, M.: The essence of the fundamental rights to privacy and data protection: finding the way through the maze of the CJEU's constitutional reasoning. German Law J. **20**(6), 864–883 (2019)
7. Brouwer, E.: Schengen and the administration of exclusion: legal remedies caught in between entry bans, risk assessment and artificial intelligence. Eur. J. Migr. Law **23**, 485–507 (2021)
8. Buchner, B., in: Kühling, J., Buchner, B.: Datenschutz-Grundverordnung, Bundesdatenschutzgesetz: DS-GVO/BDSG, 3rd edn, C.H. Beck (2020). Art. 22
9. Bygrave, L.A.: Minding the machine: article 15 of the EC data protection directive and automated profiling. Comput. Law Secur. Report **17**, 17–24 (2001)
10. Bygrave, L.A.: Minding the machine v2.0: the EU general data protection regulation and automated decision making. In: Yeung, K., Lodge, M. (eds.) Oxford University Press, Oxford (2019)
11. Charter of Fundamental Rights of the European Union, OJC 326/391 (CFREU) (2012)
12. Convention for the Protection of Human Rights and Fundamental Freedoms, Rome, 4 November 1950 (ECHR)
13. Council Framework Decision of 13 June 2002 on the European arrest warrant and the surrender procedures between Member States – Statements made by certain Member States on the adoption of the Framework Decision, OJ L190/1 (2002)
14. Court of Justice of the European Union: Case C 362/14 Maximilian Schrems v Data Protection Commissioner, ECLI:EU:C:2015:650 (Schrems I) (2015)

15. Court of Justice of the European Union: Case C-293/12 Digital Rights Ireland and C-594/12 Seitlinger and Others, ECLI:EU:C:2014:238 (2014)
16. Court of Justice of the European Union: Case C-673/17 Bundesverband der Verbraucherzentralen und Verbraucherverbände — Verbraucherzentrale Bundesverband eV v Planet49 GmbH, ECLI:EU:C:2019:801 (2019)
17. Court of Justice of the European Union: Joined Cases C-225/19 and C-226/19 R.N.N.S. and K.A. v Minister van Buitenlandse Zaken, ECLI:EU:C:2020:951 (2020)
18. Court of Justice of the European Union: Joined Cases C-511/18, C-512/18 and C-520/18 La Quadrature du Net, ECLI:EU:C:2020:791 (2020)
19. Court of Justice of the European Union: Opinion 1/15 of the Court (Grand Chamber), ECLI:EU:C:2017:592 (EU – Canada PNR Opinion) (2017)
20. Courtland. Bias detectives: the researchers striving to make algorithms fair. https://www.nature.com/articles/d41586-018-05469-3. Accessed 04 Apr 2022
21. Dietterich, T.G.: Overfitting and undercomputing in machine learning. ACM Comput. Surv. **27**, 326–327 (1995)
22. Dimitrova, D.: Data subject rights: the rights to access and rectification in the area of freedom, security and justice. Doctoral Dissertation at the Vrije Universiteit Brussel (2021)
23. Dimitrova, D.: The rise of the personal data quality principle: is it legal and does it have an impact on the right to rectification? EJLT **12**(3) (2021)
24. Directive (EU) 2016/680 of the European Parliament and of the Council of 27 April 2016 on the protection of natural persons with regard to the processing of personal data by competent authorities for the purposes of the prevention, investigation, detection or prosecution of criminal offences or the execution of criminal penalties, and on the free movement of such data, and repealing Council Framework Decision 2008/977/JHA, OJ L 119/89 (Law Enforcement Directive or LED) (2016)
25. Doran, D., Schulz, S., Besold T.R.: What does explainable AI really mean? A new conceptualization of perspectives (2017). https://arxiv.org/pdf/1710.00794.pdf. Accessed 04 Apr 2022
26. EDPB-EDPS: Joint Opinion 5/2021 on the proposal for a Regulation of the European Parliament and of the Council laying down harmonised rules on artificial intelligence (Artificial Intelligence Act). 18 June 2021. https://edpb.europa.eu/system/files/2021-06/edpb-edps_joint_opinion_ai_regulation_en.pdf. Accessed 04 Apr 2022
27. European Commission: Opportunities and Challenges for the Use of Artificial Intelligence in Border Control, Migration and Security. vol. 1: Main Report, written by Deloitte (2020)
28. European Commission. Proposal for a Regulation of the European Parliament and of the Council Laying Down Harmonised Rules on Artificial Intelligence (Artificial Intelligence Act) and Amending Certain Union Legislative Acts. COM (2021) 206 final, Brussels, 21 April 2021
29. European Court of Human Rights: Big Brother Watch and Others v the United Kingdom App nos. 58170/13, 62322/14 and 24960/15, 25 May 2021
30. European Court of Human Rights: Centrum för rättvisa v Sweden App no. 35252/08, 25 May 2021
31. European Court of Human Rights: Dalea v France App no. 964/07, 2 February 2010
32. European Court of Human Rights: Nada v Switzerland App no. 10593/08, 12 September 2012
33. European Court of Human Rights: Rotaru v Romania App no. 28341/95, 4 May 2000
34. European Court of Human Rights: S. and Marper v the United Kingdom App no. 30562/04 and 30566/04, 4 December 2008
35. European Court of Human Rights: Weber and Saravia v Germany App no. 54934/00, 29 June 2006

36. European Data Protection Board: 2019 Annual Report: Working Together for Stronger Rights. (2020). https://edpb.europa.eu/sites/edpb/files/files/file1/edpb_annual_report_2019_en.pdf. Accessed 04 Apr 2022

37. European Data Protection Board: Finnish SA: Police reprimanded for illegal processing of personal data with facial recognition software. 7 October 2021. https://edpb.europa.eu/news/national-news/2021/finnish-sa-police-reprimanded-illegal-processing-personal-data-facial_en. Accessed 04 Apr 2022

38. European Data Protection Supervisor: Decision on the retention by Europol of datasets lacking Data Subject Categorisation (Cases 2019-0370 & 2021-0699). https://edps.europa.eu/system/files/2022-01/22-01-10-edps-decision-europol_en.pdf. Accessed 04 Apr 2022

39. European Data Protection Supervisor: Opinion 3/2017. EDPS Opinion on the Proposal for a European Travel Information and Authorisation System (ETIAS) (2017). https://edps.europa.eu/sites/edp/files/publication/17-03-070_etias_opinion_en.pdf. Accessed 04 Apr 2022

40. European Parliament: Artificial intelligence at EU borders – Overview of applications and key issues. July 2021. https://www.europarl.europa.eu/thinktank/en/document/EPRS_IDA(2021)690706. Accessed 04 Apr 2022

41. European Parliament: Parliamentary Questions, Question reference: E-000173/2020. 9 June 2020. https://www.europarl.europa.eu/doceo/document/E-9-2020-000173-ASW_EN.html. Accessed 04 Apr 2022

42. European Union Agency for Fundamental Rights and Council of Europe: Handbook on European data protection law (2018)

43. European Union Agency for the Operational Management of Large-Scale IT Systems in the Area of Freedom, Security and Justice (eu-LISA): Artificial Intelligence in the Operational Management of Large-scale IT systems – Research and Technology Monitoring Report. July 2020. Accessed 09 Oct 2021. https://www.eulisa.europa.eu/Publications/Reports/AI%20in%20the%20OM%20of%20Large-scale%20IT%20Systems.pdf#search=AI%20in%20the%20operational%20management. Accessed 04 Apr 2022

44. European Union Agency for the Operational Management of Large-Scale IT Systems in the Area of Freedom, Security and Justice (eu-LISA): Call for tender "Framework Contract for Implementation and Maintenance in Working Order of the Biometrics Part of the Entry Exit System and Future Shared Biometrics Matching System". https://etendering.ted.europa.eu/cft/cft-display.html?cftId=4802. Accessed 04 Apr 2022

45. European Union Agency for the Operational Management of Large-Scale IT Systems in the Area of Freedom, Security and Justice (eu-LISA): AI Initiatives at eu-LISA. https://eulisa.europa.eu/SiteAssets/Bits-and-Bytes/002.aspx. Accessed 04 Apr 2022

46. Fotiadis, A., Stavinoha. L., Zandonini, G., Howden, D.: A data 'black hole': Europol ordered to delete vast store of personal data. https://www.theguardian.com/world/2022/jan/10/a-data-black-hole-europol-ordered-to-delete-vast-store-of-personal-data. Accessed 30 Mar 2022

47. Frontex: ETIAS, what it means for travellers; what it means for Frontex. https://frontex.europa.eu/future-of-border-control/etias/. Accessed 04 Apr 2022

48. Fröwis, M., Gottschalk, T., Haslhofer, B., Rückert, C., Pesch, P.: Safeguarding the evidential value of forensic cryptocurrency investigations. Forensic Sci. Int. Digit. Invest. **33**, 200902 (2020)

49. Galindo, J., Tamayo, P.: Credit risk assessment using statistical and machine learning: basic methodology and risk modeling applications. Comput. Econ. **15**, 107–143 (2000)

50. Geiger, R.S. et al: Garbage in, garbage out? Do machine learning application papers in social computing report where human-labeled training data comes from? In: FAT* 2020: Proceedings of the 2020 Conference on Fairness, Accountability, and Transparency, pp. 325–336 (2020)

51. Ghahramani, Z.: Unsupervised learning. In: Bousquet, O., von Luxburg, U., Rätsch, G. (eds.) ML -2003. LNCS (LNAI), vol. 3176, pp. 72–112. Springer, Heidelberg (2004). https://doi.org/10.1007/978-3-540-28650-9_5
52. Goddard, K., Roudsari, A., Wyatt, J.C.: Automation bias: a systematic review of frequency, effect mediators, and mitigators. JAMIA 19(1), 12–17 (2012)
53. Gonzalez-Fuster, G.: Artificial Intelligence and Law Enforcement Impact on Fundamental Rights. Study requested by the LIEBE Committee, European Parliament July 2020. https://www.europarl.europa.eu/RegData/etudes/STUD/2020/656295/IPOL_STU(2020)656295_EN.pdf. Accessed 04 Apr 2022
54. Google: Machine Learning Glossary. https://developers.google.com/machine-learning/glossary#bias-ethicsfairness. Accessed 04 Apr 2022
55. Green, B., Chen, Y.: The principles and limits of algorithm-in-the-loop decision-making. In: Proceedings of the ACM on Human-Computer Interaction. vol. 3, Issue CSCW, pp. 1–24, November 2019, Article No. 50
56. Green, B.: The flaws of policies requiring human oversight of government algorithms 2021. https://arxiv.org/abs/2109.05067. Accessed 04 Apr 2022
57. Hao, K: What is AI? We drew you a flowchart to work it out. MIT Technology Review, 10 November 2018. https://www.technologyreview.com/2018/11/10/139137/is-this-ai-we-drew-you-a-flowchart-to-work-it-out/. Accessed 04 Apr 2022
58. Hildebrandt, M.: The dawn of a critical transparency right for the profiling era. In: Bus, J. et al. (eds.) Digital Enlightenment Yearbook 2012, pp. 41–56, IOS Press, Amsterdam (2012)
59. Hittmeir, M., Ekelhart, A., Mayer, R.: On the utility of synthetic data: an empirical evaluation on machine learning tasks. In: ARES 2019: Proceedings of the 14th International Conference on Availability, Reliability and Security, pp. 1–6, August 2019. Article No. 29
60. Idemia, Artificial Intelligence is all around us. https://www.idemia.com/news/artificial-intelligence-all-around-us-2018-02-27. Accessed 04 Apr 2022
61. Incze, R.: The Cost of Machine Learning Projects 2019. https://medium.com/cognifeed/the-cost-of-machine-learning-projects-7ca3aea03a5c. Accessed 04 Apr 2022
62. Ingleton, R.D.: mission incomprehensible: the linguistic barrier to effective police cooperation in Europe (1994)
63. Jacobs, M., Pradier, M.F., McCoy, T.H., Perlis, R.H., Doshi-Velez, F., Gajos, K.Z.: How machine-learning recommendations influence clinician treatment selections: the example of antidepressant selection. Transl. Psychiatry 11(108), (2021). https://www.nature.com/articles/s41398-021-01224-x. Accessed 04 Apr 2022
64. Kaminski, M.: The right to explanation. Exp. Berkeley Tech. Law J. 34, 189–218 (2019)
65. Lee, M.S.A.: Risk identification questionnaire for detecting unintended bias in the machine learning development lifecycle. In: AIES 2021: Proceedings of the 2021 AAAI/ACM Conference on AI, Ethics, and Society, pp. 704–714, July 2021
66. Legg, S., Hutter, M.: Universal intelligence: a definition of machine intelligence. Mind. Mach. 17, 391–444 (2007)
67. Liao, Q.V., Gruen, D., Miller, S.: Questioning the AI: informing design practices for explainable AI user experiences. In: ACM CHI Conference on Human Factors in Computing Systems (CHI 2020) (2020)
68. Lynskey, O.: Criminal justice profiling and EU data protection law: precarious protection from predictive policing. Int. J. Law Context 15(2), 162–176 (2019)
69. Malgieri, G., Comande, G.: Why a right to legibility of automated decision-making exists in the general data protection regulation. Int. Data Priv. Law 7(4), 243–265 (2017)
70. Malgieri, G.: Automated decision-making in the EU member states: the right to explanation and other 'suitable safeguards' in the national legislations. CSLR 35, 1–26 (2018)

71. Mehrabi, N., Morstatter, F., Saxena, N., Lerman, K., Galstyan, A.: A survey on bias and fairness in machine learning. ACM Comput. Surv. **54**(6), 1–35 (2021). https://doi.org/10.1145/3457607. Accessed 04 Apr 2022
72. Ntoutsi, E., et al.: Bias in data-driven artificial intelligence systems – an introductory survey. WIREs **10**(3), e1356 (2020)
73. Palantir: Gotham. https://www.palantir.com/platforms/gotham/. Accessed 04 Apr 2022
74. Paltrinieri, N., Comfort, L., Reniers, G.: Learning about risk: machine learning for risk assessment. Saf. Sci. **118**, 475–486 (2019)
75. Pasquini, C., Böhme, R.: Trembling triggers: exploring the sensitivity of backdoors in DNN-based face recognition. EURASIP J. Inf. Secur. **1**, 1–15 (2020)
76. Poursabzi-Sangdeh, F., Goldstein, D.G., Hofman, J.M., Vaughan, J.W., Wallach, H.: Manipulating and Measuring Model Interpretability.' In: CHI 2021: Proceedings of the 2021 CHI Conference on Human Factors in Computing Systems, pp. 1–52, May 2021
77. Practitioner's Guide to COMPAS Core. Equivant 4 April 2019. https://www.equivant.com/wp-content/uploads/Practitioners-Guide-to-COMPAS-Core-040419.pdf. Accessed 04 Apr 2022
78. Rai, A.: Explainable AI: from black box to glass box. J. Acad. Mark. Sci. **48**(1), 137–141 (2019). https://doi.org/10.1007/s11747-019-00710-5
79. Regulation (EU) 2016/679 of the European Parliament and of the Council of 27 April 2016 on the protection of natural persons with regard to the processing of personal data and on the free movement of such data, and repealing Directive 95/46/EC (General Data Protection Regulation), OJ L 119/1 (GDPR) (2016)
80. Regulation (EU) 2016/794 of the European Parliament and of the Council of 11 May 2016 on the European Union Agency for Law Enforcement Cooperation (Europol) and replacing and repealing Council Decisions 2009/371/JHA, 2009/934/JHA, 2009/935/JHA, 2009/936/JHA and 2009/968/JHA, OJ L 135/53 (2016)
81. Regulation (EU) 2018/1240 of the European Parliament and of the Council of 12 September 2018 establishing a European Travel Information and Authorisation System (ETIAS) and amending Regulations (EU) No 1077/2011, (EU) No 515/2014, (EU) 2016/399, (EU) 2016/1624 and (EU) 2017/2226, OJ L 236/1 (2018)
82. Regulation (EU) 2018/1725 of the European Parliament and of the Council of 23 October 2018 on the protection of natural persons with regard to the processing of personal data by the Union institutions, bodies, offices and agencies and on the free movement of such data, and repealing Regulation (EC) No 45/2001, OJ L 295/39 (2018)
83. Regulation (EU) 2018/1862 of the European Parliament and of the Council of 28 November 2018 on the establishment, operation and use of the Schengen Information System (SIS) in the field of police cooperation and judicial cooperation in criminal matters, amending and repealing Council Decision 2007/533/JHA, and repealing Regulation (EC) No 1986/2006 of the European Parliament and of the Council and Commission Decision 2010/261/EU, OJ L312/56 (2018)
84. Regulation (EU) 2021/1134 of the European Parliament and of the Council of 7 July 2021 amending Regulations (EC) No 767/2008, (EC) No 810/2009, (EU) 2016/399, (EU) 2017/2226, (EU) 2018/1240, (EU) 2018/1860, (EU) 2018/1861, (EU) 2019/817 and (EU) 2019/1896 of the European Parliament and of the Council and repealing Council Decisions 2004/512/EC and 2008/633/JHA, for the purpose of reforming the Visa Information System, OJ L 248/11 (2021)
85. Rich, M.L.: Machine learning, automated suspicion algorithms, and the fourth amendment. Univ. Pa. Law Rev. **164**, 871–929 (2016)
86. Selbst, A.D., Powles, J.: Meaningful information and the right to explanation. Int. Data Priv. Law **7**(4), 233–242 (2017)

87. Sidiroglou-Douskos, S., Misailovic, S., Hoffmann, H., Rinard, M.: Managing performance vs. accuracy trade-offs with loop perforation. In: Proceedings of the 19th ACM SIGSOFT symposium and the 13th European conference on Foundations of software engineering, pp. 124–134 (2011)
88. Sopra Steria: Artificial Intelligence. https://www.soprasteria.de/services/technology-ser vices/artificial-intelligence. Accessed 04 Apr 2022
89. Sopra Steria: Press release "IDEMIA and Sopra Steria chosen by eu-LISA to build the new Shared Biometric Matching System (sBMS) for border protection of the Schengen Area". https://www.soprasteria.com/newsroom/press-releases/details/idemia-and-sopra-steria-cho sen-by-eu-lisa-to-build-the-new-shared-biometric-matching-system-(sbms)-for-border-pro tection-of-the-schengen-area. Accessed 04 Apr 2022
90. Statewatch: E.U: Legislators must put the brakes on big data plans for Europol (2022). https://www.statewatch.org/news/2022/february/eu-legislators-must-put-the-brakes-on-big-data-plans-for-europol/. Accessed 04 Apr 2022
91. Teoh, E.R., Kidd, D.G.: Rage against the machine? Google's self-driving cars versus human drivers. J. Saf. Res. **63**, 57–60 (2017)
92. Valverde-Albacete, F.J., Peeláez-Moreno, C.: 100% Classification accuracy considered harmful: the normalized information transfer factor explains the accuracy paradox. PloS ONE **10** (2014). https://doi.org/10.1371/journal.pone.0084217. Accessed 04 Apr 2022
93. Vavoula, N.: Artificial intelligence (AI) at schengen borders: automated processing, algorithmic profiling and facial recognition in the era of techno-solutionism. EJML **23**, 457–484 (2021)
94. Veale, M., Zuiderveen Borgesius, F.: Demystifying the draft EU artificial intelligence act. Analysing the good, the bad, and the unclear elements of the proposed approach. Comput. Law Rev. Int. **4**, 97–112 (2021)
95. Wachter, S., Mittelstadt, B., Floridi, L.: Why a right to explanation of automated decision-making does not exist in the general data protection regulation. Int. Data Priv. Law **7**(2), 76–99 (2017)
96. Žliobaitė, I.: Learning under concept drift: an overview. Technical report 2009, Vilnius University (2010). https://arxiv.org/abs/1010.4784. Accessed 04 Apr 2022
97. Zou, J., Schiebinger, L.: AI can be sexist and racist — it's time to make it fair. Nature (2018). https://www.nature.com/articles/d41586-018-05707-8. Access 04 Apr 2022

Privacy Enhancing Technologies

Application-Oriented Selection of Privacy Enhancing Technologies

Immanuel Kunz[✉] and Andreas Binder

Fraunhofer AISEC, Garching bei München, Germany
{immanuel.kunz,andreas.binder}@aisec.fraunhofer.de

Abstract. To create privacy-friendly software designs, architects need comprehensive knowledge of privacy-enhancing technologies (PETs) and their properties. Existing works that systemize PETs, however, are outdated or focus on comparison criteria rather than providing guidance for their practical selection. In this short paper we present an enhanced classification of PETs that is more application-oriented than previous proposals. It integrates existing criteria like the privacy protection goal, and also considers practical criteria like the functional context, a technology's maturity, and its impact on various non-functional requirements.

Keywords: Privacy engineering · Privacy by design · Data protection by design

1 Introduction

A decisive activity in privacy engineering is the selection of appropriate Privacy-Enhancing Technologies (PETs), for example to fulfill requirements or mitigate risks in goal-based or risk-based engineering methods respectively. While this step is highly application-specific, it can be approached systematically, since common criteria for PET-selection exist. For example, one criterion that can guide engineers in their design decisions is the privacy goal that is targeted by a PET, such as anonymity or undetectability.

Existing works have proposed different systematizations of PETs in the past. The LINDDUN methodology [11], for instance, categorizes PETs using their privacy protection goal, and differentiates between PETs that target transactional and contextual data [47]. Heurix et al. [23] categorize PETs regarding the trust scenario they target and their involvement of a trusted third party and others. Yet, these systematizations do not sufficiently take into account the practical context in which PETs are selected. For instance, they do not sufficiently consider the PET's functional context it can be applied in, as well as other practical criteria. Also, they are partly outdated.

In this short paper, we develop a more application-oriented PET classification. Our classification builds upon previous proposals, integrating some of their criteria [2,11,23], like the technology's targeted privacy protection goal, and its impact on other non-functional requirements, like the architectural impact.

© Springer Nature Switzerland AG 2022
A. Gryszczyńska et al. (Eds.): APF 2022, LNCS 13279, pp. 75–87, 2022.
https://doi.org/10.1007/978-3-031-07315-1_5

Furthermore, it includes the PET's functional context, as well as prioritization criteria, like the maturity of the technology. We present a classification of 29 PETs that we have done according to the proposed criteria.

To demonstrate the effectiveness of our classification, we compare it to the one proposed by LINDDUN based on a use case. We expect that our work supports engineers and non-experts in selecting appropriate PETs, and motivate PET developers to evaluate their technologies according to our criteria, making them more easily comparable.

2   Classifying PETs

Various approaches to selecting PETs have been proposed in the past, but their adequate application can be even more challenging than their selection, for example due to the development effort involved in applying a PET in a certain environment. Our goal is to develop an application-centered classification of PETs that anticipates the challenges that a PET can cause when it is applied. In the following, we motivate and describe the criteria we have included in our classification.

2.1   Motivating Example

To motivate the choice of criteria, we lay out the following scenario of an engineer developing an architecture for a generic privacy-friendly cloud service, assuming that it is representative for the decisions architects and developers have to make when implementing privacy requirements. This generic service allows users to register, authenticate, provide personal data to the service (e.g. names, addresses), interact with other users of the service (e.g. sending messages), and to retrieve data that is stored in the service's storages.

An engineer creates a threat model for an initial design of the service which reveals a detectability threat for the service's users: since their messages to other users are observable by the service and possibly external attackers, their relationships can be identified. A requirement is therefore elicited which states that users' messages should be undetectable. A PET that mitigates this threat has to match several criteria:

First, it has to fit the functional context of the service. This includes the targeted privacy protection goal, such as anonymity or undetectability. To ensure suitability for the scenario, however, the targeted privacy protection goal is not sufficient; also, the PET has to fit the functional requirements of the application. In a messaging scenario, for example, different PETs are applicable than in an information retrieval or computing scenario. Ideally, the PET should not only target the correct privacy goal, but should also be measurable in the achieved privacy gain. This way, a more comparable and reproducible selection is facilitated.

Second, various non-functional properties can play a role. For example, the PET should be mature enough to be applied and maintained by the development team: applying a certain technology can otherwise imply large efforts for configuration and further development of the technology. To be able to weigh different usable PETs against each other, also further properties are of interest: PETs can have an impact on the overall architecture, on the utility of transactional data, and the performance of the respective interaction.

In the following we describe the criteria we use to cover these considerations, and classify a list of PETs accordingly.

2.2   Criteria

Privacy Protection Goal. One of the most meaningful criteria for selection is the targeted privacy protection goal. To that end we use the goals proposed by the LINDDUN methodology [11], most of which have originally been proposed by Pfitzmann and Hansen [34]: Unlinkability, anonymity, plausible deniability, undetectability, confidentiality, awareness, and policy compliance.

Every PET targets one or more of these goals. Often, it is the case that several goals are targeted by one PET, since they partly overlap or imply each other. For example, it is hardly possible to achieve undetectability without also providing anonymity. In our classification, however, we usually only present one or two privacy protection goals which we consider to be targeted primarily. For example, Zero Knowledge Proofs (ZKP) primarily address the threats linkability and identifiability. While they could theoretically also be used to secretly release information, an engineer would not choose ZKP to mitigate a disclosure threat.

Privacy Metric. A technology's suitability and effectiveness need to be measurable to evaluate its added privacy gain and monitor the system over time. A number of privacy metrics are reviewed and categorized in [44]. In our classification we use these categories to connect PETs with potential metrics. Note that the broader problem of creating a metric suite that comprehensively covers the notion of privacy is a research problem out of scope for this paper (see for example Wagner and Yevseyeva [45]).

Functional Scenario. The functional context the PET shall be applied in is highly application-specific. Still, some generic categories of functional scenarios can be identified and can be used as a selection filter. We identify the following ones: *Computation, Messaging, Retrieval, Release, Authentication*, as well as *Authorization*. We use the motivating scenario above to clarify these values: a computation means that data is processed, e.g. a virtual machine processes user data to create recommendations for users; Release is the release of data to another party, e.g. a user sends location data to the service; Messaging is a point-to-point interaction between two users via n other parties, e.g. two users of the same social network communicate with each other via the service; Authentication is the process of determining the identity of a user, while Authorization is the process of determining the rights of an identified user.

Maturity. When selecting a PET, cost factors play an important role, e.g. in the set-up of the PET and in its continuous maintenance. In this paper we use the technology's maturity as an indicator for set-up and maintenance costs, since a technology that is less mature will likely have more defects and will likely imply a more laborious set-up.

For this criterion we loosely base the possible values on the Technology Readiness Level (TRL) which describes a technology's maturity on a scale from 1 to 9 [33]. We generalize this scale to 3 levels as follows: level 1 is a level often achieved in scientific work, which describes a concept and may already prove feasibility in a proof of concept; level 2 can be seen as the development and testing stage, i.e. adopting such a technology still would require considerable development effort if it is applied to a specific use case; finally, level 3 means that the technology is readily available and field-tested. Still, also level 3 may still require some set-up cost for the adaption.

Performance Impact. The performance of processes and interactions can be impacted by the use of PETs. Evaluating the performance of a certain PET, however, is not trivial, especially in comparison to other technologies. We therefore evaluate a PET's performance in a simplified manner as follows. We first generically describe the performance requirements in a certain functional scenario, and then assess if the use of a PET is expected to significantly impact the performance requirements or not.

We consider Computation and Retrieval scenarios generally to have high performance requirements: In these scenarios the user waits for the result of the interaction and will probably notice also small delays. Also, we consider Messaging to be a scenario of asynchronous communication where small increases in latency are not noticed by the users. In contrast, Authentication, Authorization, and Release scenarios generally have low performance requirements since they are usually one-time actions for which performance impacts are more acceptable.

Architectural Impact. An impact on the architecture is given if the PET requires a dedicated architectural component or modifications to the architecture, e.g. setting up a mix net requires a separate mix server. This is an important selection criterion, since PETs with this property need to be considered early on in the design process.

Utility. A utility impact is given if a PET reduces the quality of transactional data, e.g. by distorting or filtering it—and thus decreasing the data's utility for analysis and other purposes.

2.3   Classification

Table 1 shows our classification proposal according to the criteria defined above. Note that our classification only includes the so-called *hard privacy goals* [11].

Table 1. Classification of privacy enhancing technologies. A black square indicates that the PET addresses the respective goal, while a triangle indicates a negative impact on the respective criterion. AuthN and AuthZ denote the Authentication and Authorization scenario respectively.

Name	Linkability	Identifiability	Non-Repudiation	Detectability	Disclosure	Unawareness	Non-Compliance	Metrics	Functional Scenario	Maturity	Performance	Architecture	Utility
k-anonymity	■							Data similarity	Release	3 [35]			◄
Suppression	■	■						Data similarity	Release	3 [35]			◄
Recoding	■							Data similarity	Release	3 [35]			◄
Aggregation	■							Data similarity	Release	3 [35]		◄	◄
Swapping	■							Data similarity	Release	2 [24]			
Noise masking	■							Data similarity	Release	3 [32]			◄
PRAM	■							Data similarity	Release	2 [42]			◄
Synthetic data	■							Data similarity	Release	1 [1]			◄
Mix Network	■	■		■					Messaging	3 [40]	◄	◄	
Group Signatures	■	■	■					Cryptographic Games	Release	2 [25]		◄	
Anonymous Credentials	■	■						Cryptographic Games	AuthN	2 [8]			
Zero Knowledge Proofs	■	■						Cryptographic Games	AuthN, AuthZ	2 [5]	◄		
Local Differential Privacy		■						Indistinguishability	Release	2 [43]			◄
Global Differential Privacy	■							Indistinguishability	Release	2 [27]			◄
Pseudonymization		■						Entropy	AuthN, Release	3 [14]			
Deniable Authentication			■					Cryptographic Games	Messaging	3 [17]			
Deniable Encryption			■		■			Cryptographic Games	Messaging	3 [17]			
Searchable Encryption					■			Cryptographic Games	Retrieval	3 [6]			
Private Information Retrieval					■			Cryptographic Games	Retrieval	2 [30]	◄	◄	
Oblivious Transfer					■			Cryptographic Games	Retrieval	2 [7]	◄	◄	
Proxy Re-Encryption					■			Cryptographic Games	Messaging	2 [16]	◄	◄	
Homomorphic Encryption					■			Cryptographic Games	Computation	2 [18]	◄		
Trusted Execution Environment					■			Cryptographic Games	Computation	3 [26]			
Dummy traffic				■				Data similarity	Messaging	2 [46]			
(A)Symmetric Encryption					■			Cryptographic Games	Messaging, Release	3 [19]			
Steganography				■	■			Entropy	Messaging	2 [9]			
MPC					■			Cryptographic Games	Computation	3 [4]	◄		
Attribute-based encr.					■			Cryptographic Games	AuthN, AuthZ	2 [41]			
Federated Learning					■			Attacker Success Probability	Release	2 [39]		◄	

Hard privacy goals include Anonymity, Unlinkability, Plausible Deniability, and Undetectability. The *soft privacy goals* Awareness and Policy Compliance[1] are usually targeted by more generic design patterns (see e.g. [2]). There can, however, be overlaps between technologies and patterns.

Note that the maturity column includes a reference for each PET that serves as an example of an implementation or concept that demonstrates the stated maturity level. Note also that throughout the paper, we use *k-anonymity* [38] as a placeholder also for similar PETs like l-diversity [31], t-closeness [29], etc.

3   Use Case and Discussion

3.1   Use Case

In this section, we compare our classification to the LINDDUN classification which was first proposed by Deng et al. [11] and has since been updated on the LINDDUN website [47][2]. This LINDDUN classification also includes a selection methodology which is based on the LINDDUN threat types. These are connected to general mitigation strategies which in turn are mapped to applicable PETs. For instance, a linkability threat concerning a data flow may be mapped to the mitigation strategy *protect transactional data* which in turn yields the PETs Multi-Party Computation, Encryption, and others.

We use again the motivating example introduced earlier, and apply it to a social network, i.e. our example cloud service is a network that allows users to add friends, exchange private messages with each other, as well as make public posts. Note that the example used in the original LINDDUN approach is a social network application as well, making it a well-suited basis for a comparison.

We use four example threats from different LINDDUN categories, i.e. a linkability, an identifiability, and two disclosure threats, to demonstrate the effectiveness of our classification in comparison to the LINDDUN classification. These threats have also been identified (on a more high level) in an example analysis conducted by the LINDDUN authors for their social network running example, see [10]. The threats and results from the PET-selection of both approaches are described in the following (with the respective functional scenario in parentheses). Table 2 summarizes the results of the comparison.

- **Linkability (Release):** This threat concerns potential linkability of different types of transactional data which is released by the user to the server, e.g. location data and posts.
- **Identifiability (Release):** This threat describes the possibility that the server can identify the user via the transmitted transactional data, e.g. due to identifiers like name or address.

---

[1] As *soft privacy goals*, some works also use the goals Intervenability and Transparency [22].

[2] Note that we do not compare our approach to Heurix et al. [23], since they partly use different privacy protection goals and provide few selection criteria that would allow a direct comparison.

– **Disclosure (Computation)**: This threat concerns the disclosure of processed data.
– **Detectability (Messaging)**: This threat concerns the detectability of messages sent from one user to another via the server.

The LINDDUN selection methodology includes 40 PETs, of which some, however, are very similar, e.g. Onion Routing, Tor, and Mix Networks are all included. Our classification contains 29 PETs of which 13 are included in both approaches.

Table 2 shows that our classification omits several PETs that are suggested in the LINDDUN methodology. For example, in the *Disclosure (Release)* scenario, we would argue that our classification correctly omits several PETs, like Multi-Party Computation, (A)Symmetric Encryption, and Homomorphic Encryption, which are not usable to mitigate this threat: encrypting a connection, for example, does not mitigate the linkability by the server which has access to the data.

Furthermore, our classification provides more applicable PETs, e.g. Aggregation and Noise Masking which can obfuscate the relation between data and therefore meaningfully address this threat. This also applies to the *Disclosure (Computation)* scenario, where it suggests more recent PETs, like Trusted Execution Environments.

Note also how the LINDDUN methodology suggests the same set of PETs for the first two threats, linkability and identifiability in the Release scenario, whereas our results are more targeted.

On the basis of this comparison, we expect that our classification better supports engineers in the selection of PETs than existing classifications and selection approaches. This is achieved mainly by filtering through the functional scenario, but also the more targeted mapping of PETs to protection goals. Consider also that using our classification, a user can further prioritize the results using the maturity, utility, and architecture impact criteria. For example, the (a)symmetric encryption may be prioritized in the last example because it has high maturity and no impact on architecture or utility.

3.2 Discussion

Limitations. One limitation of our approach is its coverage: while it is an extensive collection of 29 PETs, it is not complete and should be extended and maintained in the future. Especially the evaluation of the maturity criterion may become outdated soon, e.g. if current research proposals are developed further.

Furthermore, the criteria we propose are deduced from a use case. Therefore, their effectiveness still has to be validated in real-world studies. Some relevant criteria, e.g. regarding other non-functional requirements, could also be missing.

Still, we expect our classification to improve the systematic selection of PETs, and the evaluation of software architectures. For instance, design decisions in software architectures can be linked to our classifications and systematically evaluated.

Table 2. Comparison of the results of applying the LINDDUN PET Selection method and our classification. Those PETs that are included in both classifications are written in bold. For example, for the linkability threat LINDDUN suggests Multi-Party Computation as a possible mitigation. This PET is also included in our classification, which, however, has not suggested it for this threat. Verifiable Encryption is also suggested by LINDDUN, but it had not been considered in our classification from the outset.

Threat	LINDDUN result	Our classification
Linkability (Release)	**k-anonymity**	**k-anonymity**
	Multi-Party Computation	Suppression
	(A)symmetric Encryption	Recoding
	Homomorphic Encryption	Aggregation
	Deniable Encryption	Swapping
	Anonymous Buyerseller Watermarking Prot.	Noise Masking
		PRAM
	Verifiable Encryption	Synthetic Data
	Feedback Tools for User Privacy Awareness	Group Signatures
	Data Removal Tools	Global Differential privacy
Identifiability (Release)	**k-anonymity**	**k-anonymity**
	Multi-Party Computation	Suppression
	(A)symmetric Encryption	Group Signatures
	Homomorphic Encryption	Global Differential Privacy
	Deniable Encryption	
	Anonymous Buyerseller Watermarking Prot.	
	Verifiable Encryption	
	Feedback Tools for User Privacy Awareness	
	Data Removal Tools	
Disclosure (Computation)	**Homomorphic Encryption**	**Homomorphic encryption**
	(A)symmetric Encryption	**Multi-Party Computation**
	Deniable Encryption	Trusted Execution
	Verifiable Encryption	Environment
	Context-Based Access Control	
	Privacy-Aware Access Control	
Detectability (Messaging)	**Mix Network**	**Mix Network**
	Steganography	**Steganography**
	Deniable Authentication	**Dummy traffic**
	Dummy Traffic	
	ISDN-Mixes	
	Onion Routing	
	Tor	
	Crowds	
	Low-Latency Communication	
	Java Anon Proxy	
	Covert Communication	
	Spread Spectrum	
	Off-The-Record Messaging	
	Mixmaster Type 2	
	Mixminion Type 3	
	Single Proxy	
	Anonymous Remailer	
	DC-Networks	

A further limitation is the potential bias in our classification since the use case and the threats which the LINDDUN analysis identifies were known to the authors before the classification was finished. We assume, however, that the bias is low since it was developed in discussion with multiple domain experts who did not know the results of this analysis. Also, we would argue that the example cases above are very generic and thus can be expected to apply to many other applications as well if they conform to the general architecture of the cloud service introduce in Sect. 2.

Criteria. Evidently, it is not guaranteed that the criteria we propose are comprehensive and that they capture what engineers require as selection criteria in practice. On the basis of the case example above, however, we expect that it works better than existing approaches also in other applications.

In comparison to Al-Momani et al. [2], we do not include criteria that indicate an impact on security and complexity, because we would argue that they are redundant. Complexity is always increased by a PET to some degree, while the actual degree of complexity is difficult to assess with sufficient precision. With regards to the security impact, there is one privacy protection goal that directly contradicts a security goal, i.e. plausible deniability contradicts non-repudiation. Thus, any PET that targets plausible deniability also counteracts said security goal, which makes this criterion redundant as well.

Comparing our criteria with Heurix et al. [23], we note that there are overlaps, for instance their *Reversibility* dimension is similar to our *Utility* criterion. The *Aspect* dimension is similar to the mitigation strategies in the LINDDUN method [47], and to some extent they are also implied in our criterion of *Functional Scenario*. Other criteria we have proposed are not considered in their approach, e.g. maturity and architectural impact.

Furthermore, previous selection methodologies do not provide means for prioritizing PETs [11,28]. In a set of potentially applicable PETs, however, we would argue it is important to have prioritization factors, such as their maturity, as we propose in this paper.

4 Related Work

4.1 Privacy by Design

Generally, our classification can be seen as a tool that supports privacy by design. As such, it is complementary to other privacy engineering methods which often assume a PET-selection without further detailing this step [20,21,37]. One such approach is proposed by Alshammari and Simpson [3] who develop an engineering process that devises architectural strategies, i.e. combinations of tactics, patterns, and PETs, to fulfill privacy goals. In their approach, the set of usable PETs is determined by the chosen design pattern. The concrete selection of a PET, however, is not specified in their work. As such, our classification could be integrated into this and other methodologies.

4.2 Systematization of PETs

Also, further works have investigated the selection and systematization of PETs. Al-Momani et al. [2] follow a similar approach as we do but focus on privacy patterns rather than concrete technologies. As explained above, patterns rather target soft privacy goals. They use the following criteria to classify patterns: applicability scope, privacy objective, qualities (e.g. performance impact), data focus, and LINDDUN GO hotspot. In this paper, we have partly used similar criteria; many criteria, however, are different since the selection of concrete technologies requires other selection criteria than patterns, e.g. maturity. Note also, that our classification of the targeted privacy objective (called privacy goal in this paper) differs in some cases from theirs. We have also proposed a selection method for PETs before, but with a limited focus on PETs that manipulate transactional data [28]. Rubio et al. [36] review 10 PETs regarding their efficiency for smart grids. Since their analysis is focused on smart grids, they also use respective classification criteria, like suitability for billing or monitoring purposes. Their work is thus complementary to ours.

ENISA has previously promoted a prototype of a PET maturity repository [13]; to the best of the authors' knowledge, however, ENISA has not continued this repository. There is furthermore an ENISA publication about Privacy and Data Protection by Design [12], as well as about Data Protection Engineering [15]. Both also classify PETs on a high-level e.g. using the properties *truth-preserving*, *intelligibility-preserving*, and *operable technology*. These, however, are not intended as selection criteria.

5   Conclusions

The selection of privacy-enhancing technologies is a task that is difficult to address systematically due to the large number of applications and functional contexts. In this paper we have proposed application-oriented criteria that support such a systematic selection, and have classified a number of PETs according to these criteria, e.g. their functional scenario and applicable metrics.

One open issue is the performance evaluation of PETs, since their performances are usually not easily comparable. Future work should therefore develop an evaluation framework for the measurement of the performance of PETs. We also want to extend our classification with more PETs, and connect them with other concepts, such as design patterns. Unifying these in, e.g., a comprehensive ontological description of privacy concepts may represent a valuable support tool for engineers. Future work also needs to show the practical effectiveness of the proposed classification in real-world applications. Furthermore, existing threat modeling tools can be extended with suggestions for mitigation based on our classification.

Acknowledgements. We thank our colleagues Martin Schanzenbach, Georg Bramm, and Mark Gall who provided their domain expertise on many privacy-enhancing technologies.

References

1. Abay, N.C., Zhou, Y., Kantarcioglu, M., Thuraisingham, B., Sweeney, L.: Privacy preserving synthetic data release using deep learning. In: Berlingerio, M., Bonchi, F., Gärtner, T., Hurley, N., Ifrim, G. (eds.) ECML PKDD 2018. LNCS (LNAI), vol. 11051, pp. 510–526. Springer, Cham (2019). https://doi.org/10.1007/978-3-030-10925-7_31
2. Al-Momani, A., et al.: Land of the lost: privacy patterns' forgotten properties: enhancing selection-support for privacy patterns. In: Proceedings of the 36th Annual ACM Symposium on Applied Computing, pp. 1217–1225 (2021)
3. Alshammari, M., Simpson, A.: Privacy architectural strategies: an approach for achieving various levels of privacy protection. In: Proceedings of the 2018 Workshop on Privacy in the Electronic Society, pp. 143–154 (2018)
4. Bab, K., et al.: Jiff (2021). GitHub repository. https://github.com/multiparty/jiff
5. Bloemen, R., Vienhage, P.: Openzkp (2020). GitHub repository. https://github.com/0xProject/OpenZKP
6. Bost, R.: Open symmetric searchable encryption (opensse) (2021). GitHub repository. https://github.com/OpenSSE
7. Centelles, A., Diehl, S.: 1-out-of-2 oblivious transfer (2020). GitHub repository. https://github.com/adjoint-io/oblivious-transfer
8. Claßen, P., Grabowski, K., Modras, K.: Anonymous credentials (2020). GitHub repository. https://github.com/whotracksme/anonymous-credentials
9. David, R., Sison, J., Vickery, J., Bundoo, K.A., Ahmed, S.: Sybil-E: LSB-steganography (2020). https://github.com/RobinDavid/LSB-Steganography
10. Deng, M., Wuyts, K., Scandariato, R., Preneel, B., Joosen, W.: LINDDUN: running example - social network 2.0. https://www.linddun.org/downloads. Accessed 14 Feb 2022
11. Deng, M., Wuyts, K., Scandariato, R., Preneel, B., Joosen, W.: A privacy threat analysis framework: supporting the elicitation and fulfillment of privacy requirements. Requirements Eng. **16**(1), 3–32 (2011)
12. European Union Agency for Cybersecurity (ENISA): Privacy and data protection by design (2015). https://www.enisa.europa.eu/publications/privacy-and-data-protection-by-design
13. European Union Agency for Cybersecurity (ENISA): Pets maturity assessment repository (2019). https://www.enisa.europa.eu/publications/enisa2019s-pets-maturity-assessment-repository
14. European Union Agency for Cybersecurity (ENISA): Pseudonymisation techniques and best practices-recommendations on shaping technology according to data protection and privacy provisions (2019). https://www.enisa.europa.eu/publications/pseudonymisation-techniques-and-best-practices
15. European Union Agency for Cybersecurity (ENISA)): Data protection engineering (2022). https://www.enisa.europa.eu/publications/data-protection-engineering
16. Colt Frederickson: recrypt (2022). GitHub repository. https://github.com/IronCoreLabs/recrypt-rs
17. Goldberg, I.: Off-the-record messaging. https://otr.cypherpunks.ca/
18. Google: Fully homomorphic encryption (FHE). GitHub repository. https://github.com/google/fully-homomorphic-encryption
19. Group, I.T.L.W.: Transport layer security. https://datatracker.ietf.org/wg/tls/charter/

20. Gürses, S., Troncoso, C., Diaz, C.: Engineering privacy by design. Comput. Priv. Data Prot. **14**(3), 25 (2011)
21. Gürses, S., Troncoso, C., Diaz, C.: Engineering privacy by design reloaded. In: Amsterdam Privacy Conference, pp. 1–21 (2015)
22. Hansen, M., Jensen, M., Rost, M.: Protection goals for privacy engineering. In: 2015 IEEE Security and Privacy Workshops, pp. 159–166. IEEE (2015)
23. Heurix, J., Zimmermann, P., Neubauer, T., Fenz, S.: A taxonomy for privacy enhancing technologies. Comput. Secur. **53**, 1–17 (2015)
24. Hundepool, A., et al.: Statistical Disclosure Control, vol. 2. Wiley, New York (2012)
25. IBM: libgroupsig (2021). GitHub repository. https://github.com/IBM/libgroupsig
26. Intel: Intel SGX. https://www.intel.com/content/www/us/en/architecture-and-technology/software-guard-extensions.html
27. Johnson, N., Near, J.P., Hellerstein, J.M., Song, D.: Chorus: a programming framework for building scalable differential privacy mechanisms. In: 2020 IEEE European Symposium on Security and Privacy (EuroS&P), pp. 535–551. IEEE (2020)
28. Kunz, I., Banse, C., Stephanow, P.: Selecting privacy enhancing technologies for IoT-based services. In: Park, N., Sun, K., Foresti, S., Butler, K., Saxena, N. (eds.) SecureComm 2020. LNICST, vol. 336, pp. 455–474. Springer, Cham (2020). https://doi.org/10.1007/978-3-030-63095-9_29
29. Li, N., Li, T., Venkatasubramanian, S.: t-closeness: privacy beyond k-anonymity and l-diversity. In: 2007 IEEE 23rd International Conference on Data Engineering, pp. 106–115. IEEE (2007)
30. Liones, E., Langille, D.: Muchpir demo (2021). GitHub repository. https://github.com/ReverseControl/MuchPIR
31. Machanavajjhala, A., Kifer, D., Gehrke, J., Venkitasubramaniam, M.: l-diversity: privacy beyond k-anonymity. ACM Trans. Knowl. Discovery from Data (TKDD) **1**(1), 3-es (2007)
32. Mivule, K.: Utilizing noise addition for data privacy, an overview. arXiv preprint arXiv:1309.3958 (2013)
33. NASA: Technology readiness level definitions. https://www.nasa.gov/directorates/heo/scan/engineering/technology/technology_readiness_level
34. Pfitzmann, A., Hansen, M.: A terminology for talking about privacy by data minimization: anonymity, unlinkability, undetectability, unobservability, pseudonymity, and identity management (2010)
35. Prasser, F., Kohlmayer, F., Babioch, K., Vujosevic, I., Bild, R.: Arx data anonymization tool. https://arx.deidentifier.org/
36. Rubio, J.E., Alcaraz, C., Lopez, J.: Selecting privacy solutions to prioritise control in smart metering systems. In: Havarneanu, G., Setola, R., Nassopoulos, H., Wolthusen, S. (eds.) CRITIS 2016. LNCS, vol. 10242, pp. 176–188. Springer, Cham (2017). https://doi.org/10.1007/978-3-319-71368-7_15
37. Spiekermann, S., Cranor, L.F.: Engineering privacy. IEEE Trans. Software Eng. **35**(1), 67–82 (2008)
38. Sweeney, L.: k-anonymity: a model for protecting privacy. Int. J. Uncertainty Fuzziness Knowl. Based Syst. **10**(05), 557–570 (2002)
39. The TensorFlow Federated Authors: TensorFlow Federated (2018). GitHub repository. https://github.com/tensorflow/federated
40. The TOR Project: Tor browser. https://www.torproject.org/
41. Unknown authors: Openabe (2021). GitHub repository. https://github.com/zeutro/openabe
42. Unknown Authors: Python implementation of post-randomisation method for disclosure control (2021). https://github.com/JiscDACT/pram

43. Unknown authors: Differential privacy (2022). GitHub repository. https://github.com/google/differential-privacy
44. Wagner, I., Eckhoff, D.: Technical privacy metrics: a systematic survey. ACM Comput. Surv. (CSUR) **51**(3), 1–38 (2018)
45. Wagner, I., Yevseyeva, I.: Designing strong privacy metrics suites using evolutionary optimization. ACM Trans. Privacy Secur. (TOPS) **24**(2), 1–35 (2021)
46. Wu, Z., Li, G., Shen, S., Lian, X., Chen, E., Xu, G.: Constructing dummy query sequences to protect location privacy and query privacy in location-based services. World Wide Web **24**(1), 25–49 (2020). https://doi.org/10.1007/s11280-020-00830-x
47. Wuyts, K., Van Landuyt, D., Sions, L., Wouter, J.: LINDDUN: mitigation strategies and solutions. https://www.linddun.org/mitigation-strategies-and-solutions. Accessed 30 July 2021

Fifty Shades of Personal Data – Partial Re-identification and GDPR

Jan Willemson[✉][iD]

Cybernetica AS, Narva mnt 20, 51009 Tartu, Estonia
jan.willemson@cyber.ee

Abstract. This paper takes a look at data re-identification as an economic game where the attacker is assumed to be rational, i.e. performs attacks for a gain. In order to evaluate expectancy for this gain, we need to assess the attack success probability, which in turn depends on the level of re-identification. In the context of GDPR, possibility of various levels of re-identification is a grey area – it is neither explicitly prohibited, nor endorsed. We argue that the risk-based approach of GDPR would benefit from greater clarity in this regard. We present an explicit, yet general, attacker model that does not fit well into the current treatment of GDPR, and give it a high-level game-theoretic analysis.

Keywords: Data re-identification · Privacy attacks · Cost-benefit analysis · GDPR

1 Introduction

Even though the European Union's General Data Protection Regulation (GDPR) became binding already in 2018, there are still active discussions ongoing about its interpretation and enforcement mechanisms. Among other notions, the core terms of *personal data* together with its counterparts of *pseudonymous* and *anonymous data* have definitions standing far from mathematical rigour.

As a result, the rules for deciding whether data should be considered personal (so that GDPR applies) or anonymous (so it does not) are heuristic and open to subjective assessment.

On one hand, GDPR Art. 4(1) gives a definition of personal data depending only on whether the person can be identified completely (even if this complete identification is indirect):

[. . .] 'personal data' means any information relating to an identified or identifiable natural person ('data subject'); an identifiable natural person is one who can be identified, directly or indirectly, in particular by reference to an identifier such as a name, an identification number, location data, an online identifier or to one or more factors specific to the physical, physiological, genetic, mental, economic, cultural or social identity of that natural person;

A. Gryszczyńska et al. (Eds.): APF 2022, LNCS 13279, pp. 88–96, 2022.
https://doi.org/10.1007/978-3-031-07315-1_6

On the other hand, Recital 26 talks about identification as a process that depends on some likelihoods, costs, etc.:

To determine whether a natural person is identifiable, account should be taken of all the means reasonably likely to be used, such as singling out, either by the controller or by another person to identify the natural person directly or indirectly. To ascertain whether means are reasonably likely to be used to identify the natural person, account should be taken of all objective factors, such as the costs of and the amount of time required for identification, taking into consideration the available technology at the time of the processing and technological developments.

Additionally, Art. 11 together with Recital 57 describe a situation where the controller's ability to identify a person may change over time. However, it is left unclear whether this change is considered to be gradual, or going from 0% to 100% or back in an instant.

In this paper we are going to study the question of the level of identifiability more closely. To put this study into context, we are going to consider identification not merely as a process on its own, but as part of an attack by a rational (i.e. economically incentivised) attacker.

On one hand, such an approach should fit relatively well into the current setup of GDPR as it is argued to take a risk-based approach to data protection [11,16]. Indeed, Art. 32 is concerned with security of processing, Art. 35 states the need and approach to data protection impact assessment, and several recitals contain further guidelines for risk assessment. However, none of them refers to any attacker models (e.g. attacker motivation, capabilities, etc.).

This observation is surprising from the rational risk analysis point of view. By omitting a well-defined goal, it will be impossible to conclude whether the protection measures taken are efficient or not. A clear understanding of the targeted attacker profiles is a necessary precondition for a rational risk analysis process [3,17].

As already mentioned above, GDPR does not explicitly refer to the possibility of partial identifiability (or related concepts like inference). Purtova [15] has reviewed the main recent interpretations of identification under the GDPR, but all of them assume 'singling out' a person one way or another. Out of the five considered typologic categories (look-up, recognition, session-related, classification and personalisation), classification and personalisation have potential to allow identification in an ambiguous manner as well. However, both of them are further explicitly limited to only give rise to identification if they point to a single person [15].

We argue that such an interpretation is too narrow to address the whole spectrum of potential privacy issues stemming from data re-identification. Of course, it is possible to take a stance that even partial identification is identification and GDPR should apply. However, as we will see in Sect. 3, under a reasonable definition, almost every dataset is partially identifiable for its subjects.

This is not just an artefact of a well-chosen theoretical construction. Probabilistic nature of data subject re-identification has been observed over and over again in practice [5,6,9]. On the other hand, identification does not have to be perfect in order to allow for attacks against the data subject. We will elaborate further on this idea in Sect. 2.

GDPR acknowledges identification as a process that involves effort and requires resources like extra data or time, (see Art. 11 and Recital 26). However, this effort is considered only in the context of identifying one person, and not as cost amortised over many subjects. As a result, it is unclear how to treat e.g. opportunistic attackers who get a hold of a dataset and try to see how many subjects they can identify without really targeting anyone in particular.

In the rest of the paper we will attempt to address the shortcomings observed above by defining an explicit attacker model and deriving a cost-benefit risk assessment framework to better understand how a data privacy target can be defined.

2   An Attacker Model

We will consider scenarios where the attacker can get full access to a dataset that has been sanitised using some anonymisation technique in preparation for the release [12]. Note that we do not cover here the techniques that limit the attacker capabilities (allowing only pre-filtered queries, forcing computations over encrypted or secret-shared data, giving access to the queries only via controlled hardware environments, etc.).

From the risk analysis point of view, the exact process of obtaining the sanitised dataset is not so important. For example the data controller may have made it available in downloadable form for research purposes [8,14,22].

Consider the scenario where the attacker does not have a prior target, but is opportunistically interested in finding out private information about some subjects.

Based on the nature of the dataset and/or the obtained information, the attacker may decide upon his further actions. In order to facilitate rational risk analysis, assume that the information carries some (financial) incentive for the attacker – e.g. it could be sold to the yellow media, or the data subject could be blackmailed.

In order to discover something interesting, the attacker invests some resources like his own time and effort to analyse the dataset.

As an illustrating example, consider the attacker's task of identifying the subject based on location data. It is known that only a few data points from mobile phone location trace are sufficient to uniquely determine a data subject [8,21,22].

However, matching a unique trace to a natural person still requires additional effort. Assume the attacker has identified a person who passes through the same locations more or less regularly. A relatively simple way for identifying this person is to physically go to the traced locations and observe people passing by at the traced times. Note that observing the same locations on consecutive days on one hand means a bigger effort investment. On the other hand it also allows to narrow down the list of possible candidates more efficiently, translating into higher identification probability for every member in that list.

Of course, the attacker does not necessarily get the list down to a single element. However, this does not mean that the attack was unsuccessful.

For our example of a financially motivated attacker, partial information is useful, too. Say, he is able to narrow the list down to g people, one of them being a well-known politician. If the initial data analysis suggests that one member of the candidate list frequently visits the red light district, the attacker can make a guess even if he has not observed the politician directly in that area. Probability of the guess being correct is $\frac{1}{g}$. If the attacker decides to blackmail the politician requesting for price p, and assuming the victim pays when the attacker guessed correctly, the attacker's expected outcome of this economic game is still $\frac{p}{g}$ monetary units.

There are two lessons to learn here. First,

Re-identification does not have to be complete in order to facilitate successful attacks.

And second,

Attacker's success in re-identification of the data subject(s) depends on the effort he is willing to invest.

Thus, in order to adequately analyse attacker behaviour, it is not sufficient to consider just a single attack scenario with a specific amount of investment. Rather, a full spectrum of possible investments and returns needs to be evaluated.

3   Cost-Benefit Considerations

From the attacker's point of view, attacking involves various kinds of costs varying from direct cash and time expenses to potential penalties [7]. For the sake of simplicity, we will consider all the costs to have monetary units in this paper. Among other things, this approach allows us to compare the costs to the potential gains of the attack.

In order to assess these gains, we need to quantify the outcome of the re-identification attack. Different measures have been proposed in the literature [5, 10,13,18,19]. In this paper, we will build on the approach proposed by Benitez and Malin [5].

They start from anonymised health datasets and match them to (semi)public records of voter lists based on sociodemographic parameters. Benitez and Malin proceed to estimate the expected number R of re-identifications and the cost C required for the analysis (which in their case means purchasing access to voter registration lists). The ratio $\frac{C}{R}$ then shows the expected cost per re-identification.

Let's augment this reasoning with benefit analysis. We note that not every re-identification is equally valuable for the attacker. Some high-profile persons are likely to yield a considerably higher outcome than most of the population.

In general, for every data subject S_i we assume a 'fair price' p_i that the attacker can get for their identification (e.g. by selling the re-identified dataset on a black market). Remember that the identification is not necessarily perfect, but may refer to a group of size g_i (achieving g_i-*distinction* in terms of Benitez and Malin). Thus the expected outcome for the attacker from the identified data subject S_i is $\frac{p_i}{g_i}$, and the total expected outcome over the whole population is

$$T = \sum_i \frac{p_i}{g_i} . \tag{1}$$

A rational attacker would only attack if this sum exceeds the cost of identification C. Note, however, that before the attack the attacker is only able to determine C, but not T, as he does not know *a priori* who the identified subjects will be, nor how small group sizes he will be able to identify. This may seem like an advantage for the party responsible for data anonymisation, but this is not necessarily the case.

Note that the attacker does not need the exact prior knowledge of T, but only the inequality $T \geq C$. An experienced attacker can make educated guesses based on his previous experience with the given type of data, the anonymisation mechanism used, and current black market prices. Assuming he runs re-identification attacks as a part of a larger systematic venture, he can also accept an occasional loss as long as he is profitable across the whole business.

We already saw in Sect. 2 that the outcome T, in general, depends on the investment C. We can now concretise this observation as follows.

The expected outcome T depends on the investment C in a monotonously increasing manner.

Justification of this claim is straightforward. If the attacker has a strategy that gives him the outcome T as a result of investment C, he still has the same strategy available with resources $C_1 > C$. This means that with the optimal strategy, he can only get a better result $T_1 \geq T$.

Even though monotonous, this increase does not have to be strict. In fact, we can expect $T(C)$ to be a stepwise function, see example depicted in Fig. 1. Some initial level of positive outcome may already be achievable with essentially zero investment (e.g. by downloading freely available public datasets and running some easy analysis). However, in order to substantially improve the result, the attacker needs a qualitatively improved approach that costs him a non-trivial amount of resources (e.g. purchasing an additional dataset from a black market). There may be several such strategy improvements until the maximal achievable level of outcome T is reached.

Figure 1 also shows the line $C = T$ corresponding to the break-even strategies. Everything above this line is beneficial to the attacker, whereas the strategies below incur a loss.

Even though Fig. 1 is just a sketch and does not correspond to any real analysis, there are two interesting observations to make here.

First,

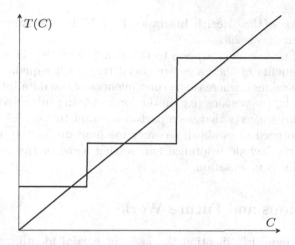

Fig. 1. Sample behaviour of outcome of the re-identification attack game

the attacker does not necessarily have just one profitable strategy, but he may have several.

Thus, in the risk analysis, it is not sufficient to cover just one or two strategies, but the whole spectrum must be considered. This is of course far from being trivial, and this is what really makes risk analysis a hard task.

Second,

if the attacker is able to achieve even a marginal partial re-identification with zero cost, and there exists a subject S_i with positive attacker profit p_i, the attacker already has a profitable strategy.

Indeed, note that in the Eq. (1) we have $g_i > 0$ for every i. Thus, if there exists a subject S_i with positive attacker profit p_i, we also have $T > 0$. We can conclude that existence of profitable attacker strategies is practically inevitable.

4   Discussion

Of course, the economic game model presented above is greatly simplified. Besides just inferring personal information, the attacker would also need to use some resources to turn this information into real profit (e.g. actually blackmail someone). Such a need incurs extra costs for the attacker both in therms of his own efforts and potential penalties. This in turn may influence the cost-benefit considerations presented in Sect. 3.

On the other hand, publishing sanitised datasets is not done just for fun, there is at least a social benefit in there, and we should account for that as well. Wan *et al.* have studied this setting and found that it is possible to find an equilibrium in this game that actually allows publishing more data than just following the default regulations (U.S. Health Insurance Portability and Accountability Act (HIPAA) in their case) [20].

There are of course more aspects to this game than just the search for equilibrium. The benefits of the game are social (e.g. higher-quality research and better policy decisions), whereas the consequences of the data inference attacks must be carried by the persons (e.g. in the form of being subjected to blackmailing attacks). This suggests that, as a part of a complete data release policy, the society may also need to establish recovery mechanisms for the breach victims. Possible measures include insurance and setting some of the extracted social outcome aside for compensation.

5   Conclusions and Future Work

GDPR fails to explicitly mention the issue of partial identification, nor does it refer to clear guidelines what to do in this case. Of course, one can take a viewpoint that even a partial identification is identification and GDPR should apply to the full extent. However, we argue that such a viewpoint is not rational as it would efficiently render any practical dataset as containing identifying data. This in turn would contradict the spirit of Recital 26 that speaks of taking objective factors (like potential attacker effort) into account when deciding about the likelihood of identification.

In practice, there are many possible levels of identifiability, and this situation should be addressed explicitly in the GDPR framework. One option would be to move away from the current binary approach where GDPR either does not apply at all or applies to the full extent. In case of partially indentifiable data, it should be possible to apply GDPR only partially as well.

It is worth noting that under the previous European data protection regulation (Directive 95/46/EC), Article 29 Data Protection Working Party released an opinion on anonymisation techniques [2]. This opinion explicitly considered the threat of inferring some partial information about the data subjects, even though no attempt was made to actually quantify the level of inference. For GDPR, similar guidelines are still in the planning phase at the time of this writing (early 2022) [1]. A position paper published in 2021 jointly by the European Data Protection Supervisor and Spanish Data Protection Agency is working in this direction stating that anonymisation is not a binary concept, and it is wrong to assume that it always reduces the risk of re-identification to zero [4].

The current paper did not propose a specific cost-benefit analysis methodology. Agreeing on one presumes a lot of discussions and is ultimately a political decision. The main message of the current paper is that this decision should take into account incentives of the actors involved. Most importantly, decisions about protection mechanisms should be based on the potential attack scenarios and not just some general rules-of-thumb.

The attack scenarios, in turn, depend on the value of the data to the attacker. This value is a continuous parameter that does not require subject identification to be 100% reliable. Even marginal success probability may be sufficient to mount a profitable attack. This consideration should be explicitly addressed by the relevant data protection regulations including GDPR.

Acknowledgements. The author is grateful to Triin Siil, Tiina Ilus, Tanel Mällo and Kati Sein for fruitful discussions. The paper has been supported by the Estonian Research Council under the grant number PRG920.

References

1. EDPB Work Programme 2021/2022, The European Data Protection Board. https://edpb.europa.eu/system/files/2021-03/edpb_workprogramme_2021-2022_en.pdf
2. Opinion 05/2014 on Anonymisation Techniques. Article 29 Data Protection Working Party, April 2014. https://ec.europa.eu/justice/article-29/documentation/opinion-recommendation/files/2014/wp216_en.pdf
3. Common Methodology for Information Technology Security Evaluation. Evaluation methodology, Version 3.1, Revision 5, CCMB-2017-04-004, April 2017. https://www.commoncriteriaportal.org/files/ccfiles/CEMV3.1R5.pdf
4. AEPD-EDPS joint paper on 10 misunderstandings related to anonymisation (2021). https://edps.europa.eu/data-protection/our-work/publications/papers/aepd-edps-joint-paper-10-misunderstandings-related_en
5. Benitez, K., Malin, B.: Evaluating re-identification risks with respect to the HIPAA privacy rule. J. Am. Med. Inf. Assoc. **17**(2), 169–177 (2010). https://doi.org/10.1136/jamia.2009.000026
6. Buchmann, E., Böhm, K., Burghardt, T., Kessler, S.: Re-identification of smart meter data. Pers. Ubiquitous Comput. **17**(4), 653–662 (2013). https://doi.org/10.1007/s00779-012-0513-6
7. Buldas, A., Laud, P., Priisalu, J., Saarepera, M., Willemson, J.: Rational choice of security measures via multi-parameter attack trees. In: Lopez, J. (ed.) CRITIS 2006. LNCS, vol. 4347, pp. 235–248. Springer, Heidelberg (2006). https://doi.org/10.1007/11962977_19
8. De Montjoye, Y.A., Hidalgo, C.A., Verleysen, M., Blondel, V.D.: Unique in the crowd: the privacy bounds of human mobility. Sci. Rep. **3**(1), 1–5 (2013). https://doi.org/10.1038/srep01376
9. El Emam, K., Jonker, E., Arbuckle, L., Malin, B.: A systematic review of re-identification attacks on health data. PLoS ONE **6**(12), e28071 (2011)
10. Elamir, E.A.H.: Analysis of re-identification risk based on log-linear models. In: Domingo-Ferrer, J., Torra, V. (eds.) PSD 2004. LNCS, vol. 3050, pp. 273–281. Springer, Heidelberg (2004). https://doi.org/10.1007/978-3-540-25955-8_21
11. Finck, M., Pallas, F.: They who must not be identified-distinguishing personal from non-personal data under the GDPR. Int. Data Privacy Law **10**(1), 11–36 (2020). https://doi.org/10.1093/idpl/ipz026
12. Kassem, A., Ács, G., Castelluccia, C., Palamidessi, C.: Differential inference testing: a practical approach to evaluate sanitizations of datasets. In: 2019 IEEE Security and Privacy Workshops, SP Workshops 2019, San Francisco, CA, USA, 19–23 May 2019, pp. 72–79. IEEE (2019). https://doi.org/10.1109/SPW.2019.00024

13. Kikuchi, H., Yamaguchi, T., Hamada, K., Yamaoka, Y., Oguri, H., Sakuma, J.: Ice and fire: quantifying the risk of re-identification and utility in data anonymization. In: Barolli, L., Takizawa, M., Enokido, T., Jara, A.J., Bocchi, Y. (eds.) 30th IEEE International Conference on Advanced Information Networking and Applications, AINA 2016, Crans-Montana, Switzerland, 23–25 March 2016, pp. 1035–1042. IEEE Computer Society (2016). https://doi.org/10.1109/AINA.2016.151

14. Narayanan, A., Shmatikov, V.: Robust de-anonymization of large sparse datasets. In: 2008 IEEE Symposium on Security and Privacy (S&P 2008), pp. 111–125. IEEE (2008)

15. Purtova, N.: From Knowing by name to personalisation: meaning of identification under the GDPR. Available at SSRN 3849943 (2021)

16. Quelle, C.: Enhancing compliance under the general data protection regulation: the risky upshot of the accountability- and risk-based approach. Eur. J. Risk Regul. 9(3), 502–526 (2018). https://doi.org/10.1017/err.2018.47

17. Rocchetto, M., Tippenhauer, N.O.: On attacker models and profiles for cyber-physical systems. In: Askoxylakis, I., Ioannidis, S., Katsikas, S., Meadows, C. (eds.) ESORICS 2016. LNCS, vol. 9879, pp. 427–449. Springer, Cham (2016). https://doi.org/10.1007/978-3-319-45741-3_22

18. Skinner, C., Holmes, D.J.: Estimating the re-identification risk per record in micro-data. J. Official Stat. 14(4), 361 (1998)

19. Truta, T.M., Fotouhi, F., Barth-Jones, D.C.: Disclosure risk measures for micro-data. In: Proceedings of the 15th International Conference on Scientific and Statistical Database Management (SSDBM 2003), 9–11 July 2003, Cambridge, MA, USA, pp. 15–22. IEEE Computer Society (2003). https://doi.org/10.1109/SSDM.2003.1214948

20. Wan, Z., et al.: A game theoretic framework for analyzing re-identification risk. PLoS ONE 10(3), e0120592 (2015). https://doi.org/10.1371/journal.pone.0120592

21. Yin, L., et al.: Re-identification risk versus data utility for aggregated mobility research using mobile phone location data. PLoS ONE 10(10), e0140589 (2015)

22. Zang, H., Bolot, J.: Anonymization of location data does not work: a large-scale measurement study. In: Ramanathan, P., Nandagopal, T., Levine, B.N. (eds.) Proceedings of the 17th Annual International Conference on Mobile Computing and Networking, MOBICOM 2011, Las Vegas, Nevada, USA, 19–23 September 2011, pp. 145–156. ACM (2011). https://doi.org/10.1145/2030613.2030630

Privacy Engineering

Google and Apple Exposure Notifications System: Exposure Notifications or Notified Exposures?

Tatiana Duarte(✉) (iD)

Vrije Universiteit Brussel, Pleinlaan 2, 1050 Brussels, Belgium
tatiana.duarte.nicolau@vub.be

Abstract. On April 2020, Google and Apple announced the launch of a joint project: a system that promised to contribute to break COVID-19 contagion chains, called Exposure Notifications (EN). Countries around the world integrated EN within their public healthcare systems. This paper provides a critical inquiry on the legal and technical architecture of EN from a data protection law (DP) point of view. It is divided in two parts. In the first part we present EN as a proximity tracking tool, along with a technical description of its implementation, and a legal assessment of the contracts established between Google, Apple and governments (or public health authorities) regarding the design of national proximity tracking applications (apps). In the second part, the findings of the first part are critically discussed in light of the concepts of 'legal by design' and 'legal protection by design', building on Mireille Hildebrandt's work. Through this conceptual approach, we examine the DP issues implied by EN's embeddings and discuss the extent to which its design reveals a defiance to the rule of law. This contribution reiterates that the fundamental right to the protection of personal data covers both our individuality and our collective heritage of democracy, the rule of law and fundamental rights.

Keywords: Data protection law · Exposure notifications system · Legal protection by design · The rule of law · Democracy

1 Part I: The Exposure Notifications System

1.1 The Exposure Notifications System Within the Strategy of Tackling COVID-19

Contact Tracing. Societies worldwide are tackling a global-scale virus whose effects are yet to be fully assessed. Our mode of living together was reshaped and is constantly being adapted to new circumstances, according to the current figures of testing, cases, and deaths. COVID-19 potential for rapid and exponential growth urges national healthcare systems to break the chains of transmission. Healthcare authorities are adopting a comprehensive strategy that includes case identification,[1] isolation, testing, care, contact

---

[1] World Health Organization [1] identifies three kinds of cases: suspected, probable and confirmed Covid-19 case.

© Springer Nature Switzerland AG 2022
A. Gryszczyńska et al. (Eds.): APF 2022, LNCS 13279, pp. 99–118, 2022.
https://doi.org/10.1007/978-3-031-07315-1_7

tracing and quarantine [1]. To fully understand the significance of Google and Apple Exposure Notifications system (EN), we first need to consider the concept of contact tracing as part of the overall strategy to contain the spread of COVID-19.

Contact tracing is the *process of identifying, assessing, and managing people who have been exposed to a disease to prevent onward transmission* [2]. In the context of COVID-19, it involves contacting each person by phone or in person to determine whether they meet the contact definition[2] and, if so, monitoring them [3, 4]. When contacted by healthcare authorities, each individual shall be provided guidance on the contact tracing rationale, symptoms to look out for and what to do when feeling unwell. It is worth mentioning that the World Health Organization explicitly states that information regarding data processing should also be provided, namely how individual's personal information will be used, processed and stored [3].

Digital technologies may be used to support rapid case reporting, as well as management and analysis of data. Distinct design proposals promised to get the most of technological progress without compromising fundamental rights. One of these proposals results from a partnership between Google and Apple (Gapple).

Exposure Notifications: Deployment and Implementation. When Gapple launched EN, they announced that it would be a two-phased project [5]. In the first phase, an Application Programming Interface (API) would be deployed to enable governments (or developers on their behalf) to develop applications (apps) within the so-called "Exposure Notifications" (EN) framework. In the second phase, the technology would be embedded in the operating system layer, so that an app would not be required for it to work. The appless system, called "Exposure Notifications Express" (EN Express),[3] was first deployed with iOS 13.7 update for iPhone.

It should be noted that the second phase does not replace the first, which means that national apps may still be operating even where the system affords to work without an app.

Public health authorities may choose among three different options: (i) keep using their app only; (ii) use EN Express without developing a dedicated app; or (iii) maintain an app while simultaneously supporting EN Express [6].

In case a public health authority develops an app, it will be available for download at Google and Apple's app stores. If it decides to offer a national app and, at the same time support EN Express (which does not require an app), the system will operate as follows: when EN is enabled and an app is installed, the system will operate with it; when an app is not installed, the system will fall back to EN Express. In any case, EN's enablement requires consent [7].

---

[2] According to the World Health Organization [2], a contact is *anyone with the following exposures to a COVID-19 case, from 2 days before to 14 days after the case's onset of illness*: (1) face-to-face contact with a probable or confirmed case within 1 m and for more than 15 min; (2) direct physical contact with a probable or confirmed case; (3) direct care for a patient with probable or confirmed COVID-19 disease without using recommended personal protective equipment; or (4) other situations of contact in specific settings, whose risk is specifically assessed. (p. 2).

[3] We did not find any contract model that regulates EN Express.

The Exposure Notifications framework uses Bluetooth Low Energy (BLE) technology to measure proximity between two devices through the strength of Bluetooth signal, a proxy for close contact, from which it is inferred that their users are presumably at risk.

To explain it briefly, individuals who (voluntarily) enable EN framework, allow their devices to broadcast Bluetooth Pseudorandom Identifiers, called Rolling [8] or Rotating [9] Proximity Identifiers (RPI),[4] to be captured and recorded by devices in the vicinity. In both designations, RPI means a random ID derived from (a Rolling Proximity Identifier Key, in turn derived from) a Temporary Exposure Key – i.e., a key that is randomly generated once every 24 h, which remains on device for up to 14 days [9]. A RPI is generated every 10–20 min to avoid identification and tracking [7, 9].

Each smartphone that participates in the EN framework stores two databases. One comprises the identifiers broadcasted by that smartphone; the other stores captured identifiers (broadcasted by other smartphones) [10].

When an individual tests positive and decides to report their diagnosis to the devices participating in the system, the database that contains the identifiers broadcasted by that device is uploaded to the app (in which case the app subsequently uploads them to a server) or, in the case of EN Express, to a server. Regularly, the participating devices check that server. If a match is found between the identifiers uploaded by a positive diagnosed person and the identifiers captured and recorded in another participating device, the device user will be informed that they were exposed to COVID-19.

Control by Design. In the EN paradigm, the generation, broadcast and collection of Bluetooth pseudorandom identifiers are ensured at the level of the operating system [9–11]. Google [9] explicitly declares that Google Play Services performs (i) the generation and management of daily random keys and RPIs (including the provision of keys to the apps for diagnosed individuals); (ii) the management of Bluetooth broadcast and collection (for instance, RPIs storage, identification of close contact with a positive case and exposure risk calculation followed by the provision of that result to the app) and (iii) the presentation of consent requests (both in the first time a proximity tracking app activates the system and before diagnosis keys are provided to the app, which will forward them to the server). These functions are not performed by national apps.

Android and iOS operating systems have a permission system that restricts access to critical resources on the smartphone, such as the Bluetooth network [10].

To perform notifications, national apps need to access the data collected by the operating system. The access to such data is performed via the EN Application Programming Interface (API), to which national apps can access only after obtaining explicit permission from Google or Apple [10].

This architecture is designed to ensure that Gapple control the major functions of the EN system. This is not inevitable. It is a design choice.

The system's functionality (i.e., the generation, collection, broadcasting and storing of keys) could be performed via national apps, which would afford public health authorities the possibility of adapting EN to their needs.

---

[4] Google [8] states that Rolling Proximity Identifiers are *derived from a Rolling Proximity Identifier Key, which is in turn derived from a Temporary Exposure Key and a discretized representation of time.* (p. 5).

We are not suggesting that such system would be a panacea or that it would be exempt of problems. The point is that, as it stands, EN is a model that guarantees Gapple control by design, where the core operations are performed by the operating system (not by an app, which in the ENE system is not even required).

Such control of EN's functionality and code grants Gapple control over implementation [10]. This is far from being of no consequence, both in terms of the application of DP law and, more broadly, to democracy and the rule of law.

Proximity Tracking. EN is designed to prevent identification by notifying the contacts of a positive diagnosed individual without however disclosing their identity nor demanding contacts to identify themselves. Therefore, EN affords proximity tracking, rather than contact tracing. Proximity tracking may be a helpful technique but does not qualify as contact tracing. This distinction might have been the reason why the protocol proposed by Gapple was renamed "Exposure Notifications", in late April 2020, replacing its previous designation, which was "Privacy Preserving Contact Tracing Protocol" [12, 13].

1.2   EN Contractual Terms *Versus* Data Protection Law: $2 + 2 = 5$?

$2 + 2 = 5$? Many meanings may be attributed to "$2 + 2 = 5$". Here, we are evoking a dialogue from George Orwell's famous novel "Nineteen eighty-four", where, during an interrogation, character O'Brien (the interrogator) asks Winston:

– *'Do you remember,' he went on, 'writing in your diary, "Freedom is the freedom to say that two plus two make four"?'*
– *'Yes,' said Winston.*

   O'Brien held up his left hand, its back towards Winston, with the thumb hidden and the four fingers extended.

– *'How many fingers am I holding up, Winston?'*
– *'Four.'*
– *'And if the party says that it is not four but five - then how many?'*
– *'Four.'*

   Winston contradicted a hypothetical dogmatic statement because his perception of reality was different than the one the interrogator was hypothesizing as one that could be imposed if the Party said so.

   In a similar way, we challenge the juridical qualification and interpretation of data protection law claimed by EN contractual terms. However, differently from what happens in Orwell's novel, it is not a (fictional?) totalitarian state imposing a dogma to a citizen, but real-world big-tech companies imposing one to States – and, therefore, their citizens.

Does EN Process Personal Data? There has been some debate on whether pseudorandom identifiers qualify as anonymous [14, 15] or pseudonymous[5] data [16–19].

It is not clear whether the different participants in this debate always mean the same thing when referring to anonymization. Sometimes, they seem to be referring not exactly to anonymization, but to the lack of effortless *identifiability*. The difference between the lack of effortless identifiability and anonymization may appear subtle, but it is highly consequential.

Identifiability relates to the reasonableness of the efforts employed to single out an individual (Recital 26 GDPR), which leads some to highlight the lack of immediate, effortless, possibility of singling out as (if it was) *anonymization*. Such account is problematic as it does not seem capable of defining what counts as *reasonable* efforts for Google and Apple.

Anonymization refers to a situation where the possibilities of singling out are in practice so remote that legal protection under data protection law is not considered necessary or proportional. That is not the case with EN.

Keys and RPIs are generated, broadcasted and collected by the operating system. The operating system also stores personal data, for instance those saved in a Google or Apple account. If Google or Apple accessed the operating system, they would have the theoretical possibility of crossing and combining Temporary Exposure Keys and RPIs with Google and Apple account data, thus making re-identification possible. That none of them will do that is a matter of trust, not of technical possibility [10, 11].

Moreover, qualifying the data processed by EN as *anonymized* would deprive individuals of the legal protection conferred by data protection law in a context where (special categories of) personal data is processed on a large scale by two big data companies.

Thus, we prefer to qualify pseudo-random identifiers as pseudonymous data.

Google and Apple: Fictional Processors, Hidden Controllers. What is the role of Gapple in processing activities within the EN framework? Are they processors as they claim to be?[6] The answer is crucial to either ascribe Gapple controller's or processor's obligations.

---

[5] EDPB [17] and ICO [18] consider that RPIs are pseudonymous data. DP-3T [19] clarifies that their protocol does not rely on anonymous communication systems to provide its privacy properties. DP-3T has considered using an anonymous communication system to efficiently query the server, but have decided against it, based on three arguments: (i) it would increase the complexity of the system; (ii) anonymity requires a trade with latency and bandwidth overhead, not being clear what the best choice would be; (iii) security properties of the anonymous communication system must be considered and choices must be made).

[6] Point 3. a. iii. GEN states that *In providing the Service, Google has no role in determining the purposes for which, or manner in which, any personal data are processed by the App.* A contrario, this means that Google denies its role as controller. Since Google provides the framework where EN operates, we can infer that Google qualifies itself as a processor. Apple indirectly qualifies itself as a processor at point 4 of AEN, by establishing that governments or developers on their behalf, as the *legal entity responsible for any user data processed in connection with the use* of their app, are *solely responsible for complying with applicable data protection and privacy laws and regulations.* Even if Gapple were mere processor, they would still have to comply with data protection law.

In this section we do not discuss controllership over data processing occurring in the operating system, which seems to be a straightforward question, as only Google and Apple decide on its purpose and means.

We are concerned with the interaction between the operating system and the infrastructures supported by EU Member-States in the context of EN and ENE, such as national apps – that is, whether Gapple are (joint-)controllers, together with governments/health authorities, concerning such data processing.

Google and Apple published separate contractual terms regulating the use and development of national apps within EN API, respectively titled as *Google COVID-19 Exposure Notifications Service Additional Terms* (GEN) [20] and *Apple Exposure Notification APIs Addendum to the Apple Developer Program License Agreement* (AEN) [21].

Despite some differences in their terms, both contracts portray a power imbalance between Gapple and governments (or public health authorities) concerning the regulation of EN.

Both Google and Apple API contracts determine that only governmental entities are allowed to use the EN API and limit the number of proximity tracking apps to one per country, unless governments have a regional approach or if Google or Apple agree otherwise.[7]

AEN states that Apple may, at its own discretion and at any moment in time, cease to distribute the national app without that implying any kind of liability.[8] It also establishes that Apple is entitled to decide whether governments are allowed to use or to remain using the EN API or its Entitlement Profile,[9] irrespective of their app's compliance with AEN and Developer Agreement terms.[10]

Gapple have a *de iure* and a *de facto* power to choose which States may develop their apps within EN API and to define the number of proximity tracking apps per country, by making it depend on their agreement. Such control is embedded by design in EN's technical architecture, but also impregnates the legal discourse imprinted in EN contracts, including on what concerns the data processing terms.[11]

The analysis of data controllership over EN requires us to evoke the distinction between 'purposes' and 'means' of processing.

EDPB [22] and, before, Article 29 Working Party [23] state that the 'purposes' correspond to the end of a particular processing operation (the 'why' data is processed), thus the entity who decides why the processing is taking place is the controller. Whereas the 'means' of data processing concern how that end shall be reached. Although some means may be determined by the processor, the decision about the most relevant ones is reserved to the controller, namely, the type of personal data that is processed, the processing duration, the categories of recipients and the categories of data subjects involved.

---

[7] Points 1. a. GEN and 2.1. AEN.

[8] Point 2.2. AEN.

[9] The *Entitlement Profile* enables the use of the Exposure Notifications API (points 2.2. and 2.3. AEN).

[10] Point 4. AEN.

[11] Point 3 GEN and Sect. 3 of AEN.

Voluntary engagement with EN by governments/healthcare authorities seems to suggest that they (at least) define the purpose of processing. However, a closer look into both EN design and AEN and GEN contracts demonstrates that Gapple, together with healthcare authorities, determine both national apps' purpose and means of processing.

Once engaged with Gapple, public healthcare authorities lose control over relevant aspects of data processing, including over the processing purposes. AEN and GEN establish that governments/public healthcare authorities may not process or disclose data using the EN API (or any other data entered by a user in a proximity tracking app) for any purpose not related to COVID-19 response efforts, such as law enforcement, including individual quarantine.[12] Such purpose limitation and specification demonstrates that Gapple (co-) determine, together with governments/public healthcare authorities, the purpose of processing.

Concerning the means of processing, the EN's contracts require governments to comply with data minimization.[13] As BLE technology does not require geolocation data to operate, national proximity tracking apps may not collect it.[14]

AEN forbids the use of location-based APIs, the collection of location data from devices and the access to identifiable information, such as photos and contacts, using frameworks or APIs in the Apple Software. The prohibition contains an important exception, though, which is: *unless otherwise agreed by Apple*.[15] If the decision of collecting further data depends on (G)Apple's agreement, either they are not processors, but, instead, controllers; or, if they are processors, such decisions may not depend on their will, and the prohibition is void.

It is curious to observe GEN terms in this regard. On the one hand, they establish that *In providing the Service, Google has no role in determining the purposes for which, or manner in which, any personal data are processed by the App*.[16] On the other hand, GEN (i) imposes governments to commit exclusively to one processing purpose; (ii) obliges national apps to comply with Google's requirements regarding consent; (iii) prohibits collection or other forms of processing, such as cross-platform association; (iv) defines precise data retention periods and (v) establishes conditions for sharing data with third parties.[17] Similar provisions may be found in AEN.[18]

Gapple present themselves as processors who genuinely want to support governments' efforts to control the spread of COVID-19, by providing a data protection-friendly system where they may develop national proximity tracking apps and verify diagnosis

---

[12] Points 1. d GEN and 3.1. AEN.

[13] Points 3. b. i. GEN and 3.1. AEN determine that a proximity tracking app may only collect the minimum amount of user data necessary for COVID-19 response efforts and may only be used for that purpose.

[14] Points 3. c. i. GEN and 3.3. AEN.

[15] Point 3.3. AEN.

[16] Point 3. a. iii. GEN.

[17] Points 3. b., i-vi GEN.

[18] AEN contemplates several similar dispositions, such as the data to be collected, transmitted, or accessed (points 3.2., 3.3., 3.4.); the use of third-party analytics and retention period (point 3.4.); purpose, the legal basis of processing and disclosure rules (point 3.1.). It furthermore prohibits processing location data; any form of data association or correlation and the access to personally identifiable information, unless otherwise agreed by Apple (points 3.2.; 3.3 AEN).

certifications from health authorities. Yet, EN is designed in a way that affords Gapple *control by design* over national apps' data processing, making of them data controllers, together with the healthcare authorities.

A similar conclusion has been held by the Belgian Data Protection Authority [24], who considered that the Interactive Advertising Bureau Europe was a data controller regarding processing within the Transparency & Consent Framework.

Joint-Controllers? EDPB [17] seems to admit that, on what concerns to data processing by proximity tracking apps, besides health authorities, other controllers may be envisaged, in which case their roles and responsibilities must be clearly established from the outset and explained to the individual users. AEN and GEN determine the means of processing by national proximity tracking apps. Such decisions are, by definition, under controller's power.

The claim that Gapple do not access any data – as it is processed exclusively on device – does not exclude joint-controllership, which would apply if Gapple were deemed to be data controllers, together with governments.

Joint-controllership does not necessarily require that each of the parties responsible for the same processing has access to personal data [22, 24–26]. What is relevant for controllership is a factual (and decisive) influence in data processing, namely by determining its purpose and its essential means [22–24].

The argument that Gapple are processors whose role consists only in providing the technical resources that afford data processing by proximity tracking apps is misleading. The party that develops a standardized system cannot always claim to be a processor, as it might in fact be controller, together with those who use the system [22, 24, 27].

We are not suggesting that the provider of a technology is necessarily a joint-controller, together with the ones under whose authority such system is used [23]. However, once engaged with EN, states lose the technical ability to make important decisions (or even participating in them) concerning data processing by their national app. This is highly relevant for assessing controllership through the lenses of the factual influence on data processing.

GEN and AEN terms allow to infer the joint participation of governments and Gapple in data processing by proximity tracking apps, making quite problematic the tenet that the latter are qualified as processors.

EDPB [22] clarifies that joint participation may result either from a common intention regarding processing, or from converging decisions by two or more entities concerning the purposes and means of processing. Decisions may be considered to be converging *if they complement each other and are necessary for the processing to take place in such manner that they have a tangible impact on the determination of the purposes and means of the processing* [22] (para. 53). Here, an important criterion to identify converging decisions is whether the processing would be possible without both parties' participation, that is, whether the processing by each party is both inseparable and necessary for the overall processing purpose. Which seems to be the case of EN, where data processing by proximity tracking apps and by the server hosted by public healthcare authorities are inseparable from the one Gapple conducts in the operating system layer (and vice-versa).

The data processing carried out by Gapple and the one undertaken by public health-care authorities are inseparable and necessary for the overall purpose of providing exposure notifications in the context of COVID-19 response efforts.

It should be noted that the contractual clauses concerning data processing only rule the design of proximity tracking apps that use the EN system, not the EN system itself.

GEN and AEN impose on Governments a specific design to their national apps, which they must abide by if they want to engage with (or keep using) their framework.

Nevertheless, Gapple qualify themselves as data processors (which, by definition, act exclusively under controller's instructions), while at the same time (i) co-determining the processing purpose; (ii) imposing a specific design on national proximity tracking apps; (iii) defining the means of data processing; (iv) imposing and perform consent requests; and (v) framing processing activities, either by permitting or prohibiting them.

The fact that two private companies determine the above-mentioned aspects of data processing in the context of a global pandemic must not be overlooked, as the exceptional nature of such context requires governments and public healthcare authorities to make decisions that impact citizen's fundamental rights and freedoms. Such decisions must be free from interferences external to the system of countervailing powers shaped by the Rule of Law.

EN's design and the contractual terms that regulate it afford Gapple *control by design* over data processing. This qualifies them as data controllers, together with governments/health authorities regarding processing performed by proximity tracking apps.

However much Gapple may, like O'Brien, attempt to impose a (legal) fiction, we may (still) freely say.

$2 + 2 = 4$ (determination of purpose + determination of means = controllership).

2 Part II: Legal by Design and Legal Protection by Design

2.1 Legal by Design

Concept. It is important to clarify what we mean by *legal by design*.

The concept was coined by Lippe, Katz and Jackson [28], who suggest that the complexity of legal relations requires human and technology ensembles to improve efficiency and accuracy in risk analysis and decision-making. As coined by these authors, *legal by design* is connoted with technological solutions that systematize complex legal information for efficient management and informed decision-making.

In this contribution, we follow Mireille Hildebrandt [29, 30], who conceives *legal by design* as a subset of techno-regulation that ensures compliance with legal norms by way of technological enforcement or nudging.

Thus, in the sense we are using it, *legal by design* is a way of forcing or nudging into compliance through design choices that embed a single interpretation of legal norms which cannot be disobeyed.

One Interpretation, (N)one Law. Law as we know it constrains human behavior with-out taking out the individual possibility of disobeying it. It speaks a language of oughts, being purposely illiterate in the vocabulary of "is" [31]. It is informed by the inherent elusiveness of natural language inscribed in text, requiring interpretation to come to life. Legal debates, lawsuits and doctrinal discussions are often about the meaning inscribed in written legal norms.

To be sure, not all legal norms *exist* through text. However, unwritten norms can be, and often are, formalized in text. Thus, hermeneutics is key to understand the affordances of text in the communication of *meaning* [32].

On a dialogue, meaning is informed by references shared among the interlocutors. Where such references fail and the *hearer* misunderstands the speaker's message, the speaker can clarify the intended meaning of their utterance. Whereas in text the message is disconnected from situated references, i.e., the *reader* cannot resort to the *author* (nor to the time and space where writing occurred) to ask what the intended meaning was [33, 34]. Therefore, the meaning-attribution task must be performed by the reader, without whom text is reduced to ink.

Text imposes interpretation, but not *an* interpretation.

Interpretation is constrained by the reader's vision of the world in the moment of reading. The finitude of human nature condemns individuals to *understand from a standpoint* which, in turn, informs the outcome of *reading* [35, 36]. Interpretation is, therefore, a generative activity[19] [32, 33, 37] where the reader is not a mere passive de-codifier of a meaning pre-embedded in text, but rather an active meaning attributor through (and in) the act of reading.

Such elusiveness of meaning in text affords (legal) argumentation and, therefore, contestation [30].

In *legal by design*, designers attribute a specific meaning to legal norms and embed it in an automated system. They choose the reading they want to enforce through automation, compile it into programming language and implement it in a hard or software solution. Contrary to text, automation imposes *an* interpretation, thereby forgetting the ductility of natural language.

A single interpretation of the law (out of many possible) is embedded in the system, enforcing or nudging individuals into adopting a specific, previously determined, course of action.

But whose behavior is being enforced through EN?

EN's design impose a specific form of processing on governments and public healthcare authorities that opt to build their proximity tracking apps within it.

Some could say that a contract presumes that the parties are in balanced positions and that governments have freely chosen to engage with Gapple's proposal. We do not know whether governments could have avoided engaging with tech-giants. We know that EN is based on the Decentralized Privacy-Preserving Proximity Tracing (DP3T) protocol, proposed by an international academic consortium, that, during sometime, supported both its own protocol and EN. However, when EN became available on most of its versions, DP3T support in the backend was removed [38].

That said, EN's design choices are not *by design* open to negotiation, let alone to alteration by the participant states, who must subject to them if they want to use EN.

It appears to be (close to) impossible for public healthcare authorities not to comply with the normative logic embedded in EN or in EN Express. Furthermore, it is

---

[19] Paul Ricœur [33] calls it *productive distantiation*.

not entirely clear how Gapple will enforce EN's contractual terms, i.e., whether they will technically block the access or the use of other platforms that would allow public healthcare authorities (as data controllers) to collect more data.

The automated enforcement of a single interpretation of data protection norms, which public healthcare authorities may not defy, seems to indicate that EN qualifies as legal by design.

PETs Approach to Design. Gapple's interpretation of data protection principles is informed (at least, partially) by the paradigm of *privacy as confidentiality* [39, 40] (which could also be called *hard privacy* [41]), that is, a design approach within the Privacy Enhancing Technologies' (PETs) field which focuses on avoiding identification – for instance, through unlikability [42, 43].

EN's design does not seem to allow public healthcare authorities, as (joint-) controllers, to collect more information than the one allowed by the system's infrastructure, regardless of whether it is necessary for the purpose of processing.

To be efficient in tackling COVID-19, healthcare authorities might require identification and further information about recent contacts of an infected person. A COVID-19 carrier with mild or no symptoms may spread the virus through their contacts and receive a notification that they have been exposed to the virus, because one of their contacts got tested first, thereby generating misleading information to the public healthcare system and to individuals [13].

Data minimization does not mean data scarcity; it means that personal data may be processed in the required measure to fulfil the purpose that determined its collection.

Ultimately, uncritical embracement of the paradigm of privacy as confidentiality may undermine the efficiency of the public healthcare systems' strategy to tackle COVID-19.

We are not saying that personal data should be collected by default *just in case* healthcare authorities might need it, but, rather, that they should be able to determine what types of data are required on a case-by-case basis.

Moreover, healthcare professionals are bound by statutory obligations of confidentiality, which makes them a trusted party to which health information may be revealed to in order to assure an efficient response from the public healthcare system.

By adopting the EN framework, public healthcare authorities commit to a single interpretation of data protection law that fosters *privacy as confidentiality* design approach, embedded in Gapple's architecture.

EN system is about avoiding identification, whereas an efficient healthcare system able to functioning on a case-by-case basis may require identification. These different conceptual insights collide in cases where the unlinkability between data and individual runs counter both the exercise of rights by data subjects and the efficiency of the whole healthcare system, as both often presuppose identification [43, 44].

As all seems to indicate, EN does not allow further data collection where necessary for COVID-19 response efforts,[20] in which case healthcare authorities are forced to comply with a (potentially inadequate) interpretation of data protection principles. That being the case, EN qualifies as *legal by design*.

---

[20] EDPB [17] hypothesises about the eventual need of processing additional data, in which case such (additional) information should remain on the user terminal and only be processed when strictly necessary and with his prior and specific consent (para. 44, p. 9).

2.2 Legal Protection by Design

Concept. The concept of legal protection by design is also taken from Mireille Hilde-brandt's work [29, 32, 45, 46]. Differently from legal by design, which is concerned with categorical rules, legal protection by design focuses on legality[21] [47] and contestability. It acknowledges that technologies have a constraining impact on human behavior that can be even more significant than the one legal norms have. Thus, automation must be subjected to the same legitimation requirements than those legal norms are as a condition of validity and enforcement within the legal order. Concretely, this means that automated solutions that impact fundamental rights must be subjected to the system of countervailing powers that shapes the Rule of Law in a democratic system.

Embedded Rule of Law. In democratic systems, representative powers are personified in the figure of the legislature, which makes laws through proper legal procedures that ensure democratic participation, or at least some form of public scrutiny. Public administration and courts' decision making must follow procedures that allow proper instances of contestation before crystallizing in the legal order [48]. This presupposes that those who wish to contest understand the logic involved in such decisions and are equipped with adequate means to challenge them.

The term *legal protection* calls for the intervention of the democratic legislator in cases where automation may impact fundamental rights and underlines the possibility of contesting its effects [29, 32, 45]. *By design* is about considering the interplay between human and machine, instead of simply embedding rules into technology by ingenious engineering [42, 46].

Gapple enforce a single reading of data protection norms via EN and impose such reading on the governments that engage with it. By such engagement, countries let Gapple be the interpreter and the executor of legal norms through automation, voiding their power as a publicly accountable sovereign in favor of private companies that dominate digital infrastructure. Contrary to governments, private companies are not constrained by the substantial, formal and procedural norms that shape the Rule of Law (at least not in the way governments are) [49].

The effect of EN is particularly problematic, as its legal and technical infrastructure have a normative effect in the way countries (un)protect fundamental rights, such as the right to protection of personal data and the right to respect for private life, provided for in Articles 7 and 8 of Charter of Fundamental Rights of the European Union.

Let us take a look into the means by which legal protection may be ensured by design and the extent to which EN does (not) afford them.

DPIA and Data Protection by Design and by Default. The use of a new technology likely to result in a high risk to the rights and freedoms of natural persons requires data controllers to conduct a Data Protection Impact Assessment (DPIA), under Article 35 (1) GDPR. Recital (75) GDPR provides interpretative hints for understanding what the European legislator means by *risk to the rights and freedoms of natural persons*.

---

[21] By using the term legality, we are invoking the meaning stated in [46].

In particular, a DPIA is mandatory where health data is processed – which unequivocally happens in the case of diagnosis keys – on a large scale (Article 35 (3) (b) GDPR).

Proximity tracking apps process data under the constraints imposed by EN's legal and technical infrastructure. The way that EN enforces the purpose and means of processing by proximity tracking apps was a design decision by Gapple, which makes of them joint-controllers, together with healthcare authorities, concerning the data processing performed by such apps. Such circumstance dictates Gapple's legal obligation of conducting a DPIA regarding the aspects of processing under their control.

This does not mean that public healthcare authorities are exempt from performing a DPIA. Indeed, they are obliged to do so in the exact measure of their data processing controllership.

Yet, our point is that Gapple's influence on the determination of the purpose and means of processing by national apps should have been preceded by a DPIA. Ideally, Gapple and healthcare authorities should have developed their DPIAs together or, more realistically, the latter should have based their DPIA on the one conducted by the former. We do not know whether healthcare authorities have benefitted from Gapple's input while conducting their DPIAs.

A DPIA must identify and assess risks to rights and interests of natural persons and mitigate them through the implementation of security mechanisms that ensure compliance with the GDPR. Such security measures call for Article 32 GDPR, but also for data protection by design and by default, stated in Article 25 GDPR, which requires a thorough balance between the circumstances and risks of processing and individual's rights and interests, and the mitigation by default of potentially negative consequences that may derive from data processing.

The thorough balance required by Article 25 GDPR is not sufficiently addressed by data controllers by simply embedding a design paradigm, such as privacy as confidentiality, without spelling out the trade-offs and reasons for such choice.

Articles 25 and 35 GDPR are not about brute (en)forcing a one-eyed interpretation of a norm; rather, they acknowledge the complexity and delicacy of the equilibrium required for compliance with data protection law. Their practical effect must be to empower natural persons to contest the product of automation.

A DPIA would allow informed decisions [50][22] both by the democratic legislator (before opting in to the EN system) and citizens (before downloading a national app functioning within EN framework or before enabling EN Express on their devices and, in case of a positive test, before uploading their keys to the app/server).

In this regard, Gapple's lack of transparency seems to be quite transparent.

The Right to Obtain Human Intervention. When covered by Article 22 GDPR, access to healthcare is worthy of attention [51].

In the context of Gapple EN, Article 22 GDPR applies to the risk scoring attributed by the system. This is not a univocal position. For instance, the data protection statement

---

[22] World Health Organization homepage [50] explicitly states that transparency and explainability apply to the operation of apps and application programming interfaces (APIs) of COVID-19 proximity tracking technologies. (p. 3).

of the Belgian app *Corona alert* [52] explicitly states that *The Contact Tracing App does not take any automated decisions with regard to a user within the meaning of article 22 of the General Data Protection Regulation*. However, it seems clear that the automated attribution of risk score in the context of an infectious disease such as COVID-19 may have a significant impact on individual's lives – and, therefore, Article 22 GDPR must apply.

Let us look into the risk score attribution process.

The EN design allows healthcare authorities to get an exposure risk scoring by matching the collected keys and computing exposure data in the form of ExposureWindow[23] object [53]. The risk score associated with the ExposureWindow may be precalculated, or manually calculated.[24]

To get precalculated risk scores, the app must retrieve the diagnosis keys from the server and then provide them to the EN system. The precalculated risk score is obtained by calculating each ExposureWindow, aggregated into DailySummary[25] objects for the last 14 days of exposure data. In the case of manual calculation,[26] the getExposureWindows() method provides the exposures matching the diagnosis keys, from which the risk score is calculated [53]. This method affords public healthcare authorities more control over the risk score calculation process [53].

Data subjects are entitled not to be subject to automated individual decision-making, where such decisions impact them in a relevant way (Article 22 (1) GDPR). However, automated decision-making may be performed where it is (i) necessary to enter into a contract, (ii) authorized by EU or Member-State law, or (iii) based on data subject's explicit consent (Article 22 (2) GDPR).

---

[23] Each ExposureWindow instance represents up to 30 min of exposure information. As a result, longer exposures to a particular key might be split into multiple 30-min blocks.

[24] By using the word *manual*, we are adopting Google's [53] terminology. This should not be taken as implying automation absence, as risk score calculation remains an automated process. We suspect that by *manual*, Google means that health authorities have (more) control of the risk scoring method.

[25] Each DailySummary contains the ExposureSummaryData for a particular day. The ExposureSummaryData takes into account the highest risk score, looking at all ExposureWindows aggregated into the summary; a sum of the risk scores and a sum of the weighted durations for all ExposureWindows.

[26] Google [53] provides an example of how to manually compute the risk score, which considers three factors: (i) weighted minutes-at-attenuation; (ii) infectiousness weight (available only for v1.6 and later); (iii) report type weight. The method exemplified by Google iterates through the list of ExposureWindow objects retrieved from the API. For each ExposureWindow, it calculates the risk score based on how many seconds a person (i.e., the device) has been within close distance of someone (i.e., another device) that reported a case. The resulting window score is added to the corresponding day score. The result is a map of dates with user exposures, measured in seconds. The code uses a filter to remove days with less than 15 min of relevant exposure. Such method computes the risk score similarly to how the Exposure Notifications system computes daily summaries. The method iterates over the different ScanInstance objects (corresponding to a few seconds during which a beacon with the diagnosis key causing this exposure was observed) and calculates the score based on the duration of the scan and the multiplier values associated with attenuation, report type, and infectiousness.

Participation in the EN system implies that smartphones *listen* and store keys broadcasted by other devices, which requires consent, under Article 5 (1) of E-privacy Directive [17].

An interesting issue is whether requiring consent for storing or accessing information stored in the smartphone necessarily means that consent is the legal ground for data processing (for whatever legitimate purpose). To be sure, Recital (17) of E-privacy Directive states that the meaning of *consent* is the same as the one provided for in the Directive 95/46 (now GDPR), which seems to indicate that consent is as much a legal ground in the E-privacy Directive as it is in the GDPR.

However, that would mean that every single instance of data processing involving information stored or to be stored on smartphones (or on any terminal equipment) would necessarily be grounded on consent. Although that might often be the case, such interpretative restriction seems off key, as consent is not always the most adequate legal ground for data processing.

It might, therefore, be pertinent to distinguish between guaranteeing explicit authorization on the part of the data subject to access their devices (i.e., consent) and the subsequent processing legal ground. Indeed, that happened in practice.

Some countries distinguish individual authorization from the subsequent processing legal ground. That is the case of the Belgian app [52]. As it operates under EN protocols, data subjects are always asked for consent for enabling EN on their devices and for uploading their exposure keys to (the app, which shares it with) a national the server. Nevertheless, the processing legal ground adopted by the Belgian app is not consent. Rather, processing activities performed for notifying and registering devices on EN are grounded on public interest (Article 6 (1) (e) GDPR) and, where they involve health data, on public interest in the area of public health (Article 9 (2) (i) GDPR) [52].

Where diagnosis keys are uploaded, health data is processed. According to Article 22 (4) GDPR, that can only happen under consent or for reasons of substantial public interest, on the basis of Union or Member State law (respectively, Article 9 (1) (a) and (g) GDPR).

An in-depth study on the most adequate processing legal ground is out of the scope of this article, but it is relevant to point out the complexity of this question when examining the applicability of Article 22 GDPR to EN.

This kind of interpretative difficulties can be more a feature than a bug if we *read* them as favoring a broader and deeper level of protection of fundamental rights of natural persons.

Participating on EN is an individual act with public interest relevance. The two-dimensional nature of this kind of processing should summon the typical safeguards provided both by consent and by public interest-based processing – even where we consider that *voluntary participation* is different from *consent* as a processing legal basis, or that *substantial public interest* is technically different from *public interest in the area of public health*.

How can this be done coherently and in a way that respects the integrity of data protection law?

Where processing is based on consent, Article 22 (3) GDPR consecrates the data subjects' right to obtain human intervention on the part of the controller, to express their point of view and to contest the decision. This right implies that specific information is provided to data subjects, both *ex ante*, about the logic involved in decision-making process (Articles 13 (2) (f); 14 (2) (g); 15 (1) (h) of the GDPR), and *ex post*, by a human being, who will necessarily intervene and (at least) consider data subject's point of view (Recital 71 of the GDPR). Such safeguards should apply to data processing in the context of risk score attribution, even where the legal ground is public interest in the area of public health (rather than consent).

Although they must be technically distinguished, the affinities between voluntary participation on EN and consent seem to justify extending the safeguards provided for consent-based processing, even where consent is not considered to be the processing legal ground, as is the case in Belgium. Such is the result of prioritizing legal protection over legal certainty concerning processing legal grounds.

We are aware that the lack of legal certainty has a deterring effect on data controllers. Thus, we are not suggesting a generic dismissal of legal certainty in favor of protection, as they are not always antinomic. The prioritization of legal protection over legal certainty in the context of EN is rooted on the categories of data controllers involved in processing, that is, big tech companies and states. Albeit very different in nature, they have something in common, which is that they are particularly obliged (in the case of governments) and well equipped (for instance, in terms of budget and resources) to ensure legal protection, which binds them to guarantee a high(er) level of protection to personal data.

A different issue is exercise of rights in the context of risk-score attribution. Risk-score calculation may either be the result of Gapple's (precalculated) formula or national health authority's formula. The entity that decided on the applicable formula is obliged to provide information about the logic involved in the calculation method, and to respond to data subjects' requests who want to exercise their rights.

Mireille Hildebrandt [29] considers that the obligation to conduct a DPIA, the requirements of data protection by design and by default and the right not to be subject to a decision based solely on automated processing are instances of *legal protection by design* in the GDPR.

None of them seems to be (fully) guaranteed by EN.

Addressing fundamental rights issues that emerge on technological environments requires the willingness to approach them in a multi and cross disciplinary way. Policy makers must count on computer scientists to navigate the aptitude and the limitations of automation where fundamental rights might be impacted by it. Conversely, computer scientists must count on lawyers to understand the modes of veridiction of law [54] in order to create sustainable solutions, in line with the Rule of Law.

Future work must not overlook the insufficiency of a single discipline when addressing technologies with social impact.

3 Epilogue: From Data Protection to the Rule of Law

This contribution provides a critical review of the EN system, opening alleys to reflect on the power relations between governments and the companies who control the communications infrastructure, as well as about democratic participation in the process of deploying new technologies and the means of contesting their outcome.

A data protection analysis of EN incited us to muse around its impact on the Rule of Law and fundamental rights.

Gapple's control over data processing is reflected both in EN's embeddings and in their legal discourse as contractual parties.

The operating system affords Gapple control not only over the system itself, but also over the exposure data. By controlling the exposure data, they get to determine how public healthcare systems manage proximity tracking within their overall public healthcare strategy.

At the same time that Gapple imposes on governments a specific design and a static form of data processing for proximity tracking, they present themselves as processors that are only providing the tools to support COVID-19 combating efforts.

Companies' decision-making is not supported by procedures that aim to treat people with equal concern and respect [55], nor by institutions who are bound to decide according to standards of proportionality, legal certainty and purposiveness [56]. In the big-tech world, e-suzerains[27] seem to rule [57].

The power imbalance between governments, as citizens representatives, and Gapple is particularly worrying in the context of the outbreak of a global virus. But the worrying factor does not disappear once COVID-19 is tackled. Through the embedment of EN in devices, Gapple created a potential mass surveillance functionality, whose use after COVID-19 outbreak is unknown [10].

To state that Gapple's proposal does not provide legal protection by design is not just a theoretical exercise of conceptual fitness. It is something that affects the heart of our political systems and the concept of law itself.

To be (dis)continued.

Acknowledgements. I would like to express my deepest appreciation to Jaap-Henk Hoepman (Radboud University Nijmegen, University of Groningen) for his invaluable contribution in making a technical review of this paper, pointing out aspects that eluded me, which has majorly improved its technical rigor and soundness.

References

1. Word Health Organization homepage: COVID-19 Case definition, 16 December 2020. https://www.who.int/publications/i/item/WHO-2019-nCoV-Surveillance_Case_Definition-2020.2. Accessed 26 Jan 2022
2. Word Health Organization homepage: Contact tracing in the context of COVID-19, Interim guidance, 10 May 2021. https://apps.who.int/iris/bitstream/handle/10665/332049/WHO-2019-nCoV-Contact_Tracing-2020.1-eng.pdf?sequence=1&isAllowed=y. Accessed 26 Jan 2022
3. Word Health Organization homepage: Contact tracing in the context of COVID-19, Interim guidance, 1 February 2021. https://www.who.int/publications/i/item/contact-tracing-in-the-context-of-covid-19. Accessed 26 Jan 2022

---

[27] The epithet suzerain, used as metaphor in this context, intends to stress Gapple's lack of institutional framework, infused by an idea of personal power (in the case, concentration of power in certain categories of private entities). I took inspiration from Mireille Hildebrandt [55].

4. Word Health Organization homepage: Considerations for quarantine of contacts of COVID-19 cases Interim guidance, 25 June 2021. https://www.who.int/publications/i/item/WHO-2019-nCoV-IHR-Quarantine-2021.1. Accessed 26 Jan 2022
5. Google homepage: Exposure Notification, Frequently Asked Questions, Preliminary – Subject to Modification and Extension v1.0, April 2020. https://blog.google/documents/63/Exposure_Notification_-_FAQ_v1.0.pdf. Accessed 26 Jan 2022
6. Apple homepage: Supporting Exposure Notifications Express. https://developer.apple.com/documentation/exposurenotification/supporting_exposure_notifications_express. Accessed 26 Jan 2022
7. Google homepage: Exposure Notifications Frequently Asked Questions Preliminary – Subject to Modification and Extension v. 1.2, September 2020. https://static.googleusercontent.com/media/www.google.com/en//covid19/exposurenotifications/pdfs/Exposure-Notification-FAQ-v1.2.pdf. Accessed 26 Jan 2022
8. Google homepage: Exposure Notification Cryptography Specification Preliminary, April 2020. https://blog.google/documents/69/Exposure_Notification_-_Cryptography_Specification_v1.2.1.pdf. Accessed 29 Jan 2022
9. Google homepage: Exposure Notifications API. https://developers.google.com/android/exposure-notifications/exposure-notifications-api. Accessed 16 Jan 2022
10. Hoepman, J-H.: A Critique of the Google Apple Exposure Notification (GAEN) Framework, 12 January 2021. https://arxiv.org/pdf/2012.05097.pdf. Accessed 22 Jan 2022
11. Leith, D., Farrell, S.: Contact tracing app privacy: what data is shared by Europe's GAEN contact tracing apps, 18 July 2020. https://www.scss.tcd.ie/Doug.Leith/pubs/contact_tracing_app_traffic.pdf. Accessed 29 Sept 2020
12. Google homepage: Privacy Preserving Contact Tracing Protocol. https://covid19.apple.com/contacttracing. Accessed 29 Jan 2022
13. Bunnie Studios (blog): On Contact Tracing and Hardware Tokens (Bunnie studios), May 2020. https://www.bunniestudios.com/blog/?p=5820. Accessed 29 Jan 2022
14. WeHealth homepage. https://www.wehealth.org/arizona. Accessed 16 Jan 2022
15. National Health Service homepage: Guidance NHS COVID-19 app: anonymization, definitions and user data journeys, 1 October 2020. https://www.gov.uk/government/publications/nhs-covid-19-app-privacy-information/anonymisation-definitions-and-user-data-journeys. Accessed 16 Jan 2022
16. Bradford, L., Aboy, M., Liddell, K.: COVID-19 contact tracing apps: a stress test for privacy, the GDPR, and data protection regimes. J. Law Biosci. 7(1), 1–21 (2020). https://doi.org/10.1093/jlb/lsaa034
17. EDPB: Guidelines 04/2020 on the use of location data and contact tracing tools in the context of the COVID-19 outbreak, 21 April 2020
18. ICO: COVID-19 contact tracing: data protection expectations on app development, 4 May 2020
19. DP-3T: Clarified anonymous communication question, posted by Carmela Troncoso on Github, 7 April 2020. https://github.com/DP-3T/documents/commit/f9c5ba50726652f914869dab8ebf07877aa4a81d#diff-c7bd425fd98aad1f9fef20099637bcbdcfadeb566ba1f83bb40ce484f195b8cf. Accessed 31 Mar 2022
20. Google COVID-19 Exposure Notifications Service Additional Terms. https://blog.google/documents/72/Exposure_Notifications_Service_Additional_Terms.pdf. Revised 4 May 2020. Accessed 26 Mar 2022
21. Apple Exposure Notification APIs Addendum to the Apple Developer Program License Agreement. https://developer.apple.com/contact/request/download/Exposure_Notification_Addendum.pdf. Revised 4 May 2020. Accessed 26 Mar 2022
22. EDPB: Guidelines 07/2020 on the concepts of controller and processor in the GDPR (Version 1.0), 2 September 2020

23. Article 29 Working Party: Opinion 1/2010 on the concepts of "controller" and "processor", (WP 169), 16 February 2010
24. Belgian Data Protection Authority, Decision on the merits 21/2022 on case number DOS-2019-01377 (Unofficial translation from Dutch), 2 February 2022. https://www.gegevensbesc hermingsautoriteit.be/publications/beslissing-ten-gronde-nr.-21-2022-english.pdf. Accessed 4 Jan 2022
25. C-25/17 Jehovan todistajat (ECLI:EU:C:2018:551) (2018)
26. C-210/16 Wirtschaftsakademie (ECLI:EU:C:2018:388) (2018)
27. C-40/17 Fashion ID (ECLI:EU:C:2019:629) (2019)
28. Lippe, P., Katz, D., Jackson, D.: Legal by design: a new paradigm for handling complexity in banking regulation and elsewhere in law. Oregon Law Rev. **93**(4), 833–852 (2015)
29. Hildebrandt, M.: Law for Computer Scientists and Other Folk. OUP (2020)
30. Hildebrandt, M.: Legal and technological normativity: more (and less) than twin sisters. Techné: Res. Philos. Technol. **12**(3), 169–183 (2008)
31. Brownsword, R.: Technological management and the rule of law. Law Innov. Technol. **8**(1), 100–140 (2016). https://doi.org/10.1080/17579961.2016.1161891
32. Hildebrandt, M.: Smart Technologies and the End(s) of Law. Edward Elgar Publishing, Cheltenham (2015)
33. Ricœur, P.: Speaking and writing. In: Interpretation Theory: Discourse and the Surplus of Meaning, pp. 25–44. Texas University Press (1976)
34. Ricœur, P.: The model of the text: meaningful action considered as text. In: New Literary History, vol. 5, no. 1, pp. 91–117. What Is Literature? The Johns Hopkins University Press (1973). https://doi.org/10.2307/468410
35. Gadamer, H.-G.: Truth-and-Method, Second, Revised Edition Translation revised by Joel Weinsheimer and Donald G. Mars, Continuum (2004)
36. Fish, S · Is There a Text in This Class? The Authority of Interpretive Communities. Harvard University Press (1980)
37. Hildebrandt, M.: Text-driven jurisdiction in cyberspace. In: Keynote Hart Workshop–New Perspectives on Jurisdiction and the Criminal Law, April 2021
38. GitHub homepage. https://github.com/DP-3T/dp3t-sdk-backend. Accessed 18 Mar 2022
39. Gürses, S.: Can you engineer privacy?. Commun. ACM **57**(8) (2014). https://doi.org/10.1145/2633029
40. Danezis, G., Gürses, S.: A critical review of 10 years of Privacy, 1–16, August 2010. https://homes.esat.kuleuven.be/~sguerses/papers/DanezisGuersesSurveillancePets2010.pdf. Accessed 21 Mar 2022
41. Danezis, G.: Distributed ledgers: what is so interesting about them? Conspicuous chatter (blog), 27 September 2018. https://conspicuouschatter.wordpress.com/2018/09/27/distri buted-ledgers-what-is-so-interesting-about-them/. Accessed 21 Mar 2022
42. Hoepman, J.-H.: Privacy design strategies (extended abstract). In: 6th Annual Privacy Law Scholars Conference, Berkeley, June 2013
43. Hoepman, J.-H.: Privacy is Hard and Seven Other Myths – Achieving Privacy Through Careful Design. MIT (2021)
44. Veale, M., Binns, R., Ausloos, J.: When data protection by design and data subject rights clash. Int. Data Privacy Law **8**(2), 105–123 (2018). https://doi.org/10.1093/idpl/ipy002
45. Hildebrandt, M.: Law as computation in the era of artificial legal intelligence: speaking law to the power of statistics. Univ. Toronto Law J. **68**(Supplement 1), 12–35 (2018). https://doi.org/10.3138/utlj.2017-0044
46. Hildebrandt, M.: Legal protection by design. Objections and refutations. Legisprudence **5**(2), 223–248 (2011). https://doi.org/10.5235/175214611797885693
47. Hildebrandt, M.: Radbruch's Rechtsstaat and Schmitt's legal order: Legalism, Legality and the Institution of Law. New Hist. Jurisprud. Hist. Anal. Law **2**(1), 42–63 (2015)

48. Waldron, J.: The Rule of law and the importance of procedure. In: Nomos **50**, 3–31 (2011)
49. Diver, L.: Digisprudence: the design of legitimate code. Law Innov. Technol. **13**(2), 325–364 (2021). https://doi.org/10.1080/17579961.2021.1977217
50. Word Health Organization homepage: Ethical considerations to guide the use of digital proximity tracking technologies for COVID-19 contact tracing (Interim guidance), 28 May 2020, https://www.who.int/publications/i/item/WHO-2019-nCoV-Ethics_Contact_trac ing_apps-2020.1. Accessed 29 Jan 2022
51. Article 29 Working Party: Guidelines on Automated individual decision-making and Profiling for the purposes of Regulation 2016/679 (WP 251), 6 February 2018
52. Coronalert Privacy statement. https://coronalert.be/en/privacy-statement/. Accessed 19 Mar 2022
53. Google homepage: Define meaningful exposures. https://developers.google.com/android/exp osure-notifications/meaningful-exposures. Accessed 22 Jan 2022
54. Latour, B.: An Inquiry to the Modes of Existence – An Anthropology of the Moderns, Translated by Catherine Porter. Harvard University Press, Cambridge (2013)
55. Dworkin, R.: Reply to Paul Ricœur. Ratio Juris **7**(3) 287–290 (1994)
56. Radbruch, G.: Legal philosophy. In: Legal Philosophies of Lask, Radbruch, and Dabin. Wilk, K., (trans.). Harvard University Press (1950)
57. Hildebrandt, M.: Origins of the criminal law: punitive interventions before sovereignty. In: Dubber, M.D. (ed.) Foundational Texts in Modern Criminal Law, pp. 219–238. Ch. 11. Oxford University Press (2014). https://doi.org/10.1093/acprof:oso/9780199673612.001.0001

Analysis and Constructive Criticism of the Official Data Protection Impact Assessment of the German Corona-Warn-App

Rainer Rehak[1]([⊠]) [iD], Christian R. Kühne[2], and Kirsten Bock[3]

[1] Weizenbaum Institute for the Networked Society, Hardenbergstraße 32, 10623 Berlin, Germany
rainer.rehak@wzb.eu
[2] Forum Computer Scientists for Peace and Societal Responsibility, Goetheplatz 4, 28203 Bremen, Germany
[3] Independent Centre for Privacy Protection Schleswig-Holstein (ICPP), Postbox 71 16, 24171 Kiel, Germany

Abstract. On June 15, 2020, the official data protection impact assessment (DPIA) for the German Corona-Warn-App (CWA) was made publicly available. Shortly thereafter, the app was made available for download in the app stores. However, the first version of the DPIA had significant weaknesses, as this paper argues. However since then, the quality of the official DPIA increased immensely due to interventions and interactions such as an alternative DPIA produced by external experts and extensive public discussions. To illustrate the development and improvement, the initial weaknesses of the official DPIA are documented and analyzed here. For this paper to meaningfully do this, first the purpose of a DPIA is briefly summarized. According to Article 35 of the GDPR, it consists primarily of identifying the risks to the fundamental rights and freedoms of natural persons. This paper documents at least specific methodological, technical and legal short-comings of the initial DPIA of the CWA: 1) It only focused on the app itself, neither on the whole processing procedure nor on the infrastructure used. 2) It only briefly touched on the main data protection specific attacker, the processing organization itself. And 3) The discussion of effective safeguards to all risks including such as the ones posed by Google and Apple has only insufficiently been worked out. Finally, this paper outlines the constructive criticism and suggestions uttered, also by the authors of this paper, regarding the initial release. As of now, some of those constructive contributions have been worked into the current DPIA, such as 1) and 2), but some central ones still haven't, such as 3). This paper aims to provide an opportunity to improve the practical knowledge and academic discourse regarding high-quality DPIAs.

Keywords: Data protection · Data protection impact assessment · DPIA · Corona apps · CWA · Digital contact tracing · Decentralization · GDPR · Privacy

© Springer Nature Switzerland AG 2022
A. Gryszczyńska et al. (Eds.): APF 2022, LNCS 13279, pp. 119–134, 2022.
https://doi.org/10.1007/978-3-031-07315-1_8

1 Introduction

After Germany opted for a data protection friendly, decentralized approach to automated, app-based digital contact tracing, the Corona-Warn-App (CWA) [1] was released by the Robert Koch-Institute on June 16, 2020. A technically outstanding system was created within a short period of time by the contractors SAP and T-Systems. It uses current software frameworks, is open source software and was partly created with transparent participatory work processes even building up a lively community. In this process, criticism from the general public as well as contributions from IT and data protection experts were taken into account in many cases. Now it remains to be hoped that a new standard has been established for future governmental IT projects in Germany. Of course, the CWA is not without data protection issues [2].

The CWA's publication was accompanied by a comprehensive Data Protection Impact Assessment (DPIA) according to Art. 35 GDPR [3], which is mandatory for such societally impactful projects. The official DPIA recognizes many critical data protection issues of the CWA, but also ignores others.

Although the idea of DPIAs has generally been around for years and the methodology gets more and more elaborated [4], actual DPIAs are usually not published. In addition, Corona apps are a novel technology and so only two related works can be named here. First there is the independent model DPIA for CWA presented by a group of researchers (including the authors of this paper) from an NGO called Forum Computer Scientists for Peace and Societal Responsibility on April 14, 2020 (FIfF DPIA) [5] and second, there is the excellent DPIA for the Austrian Stopp Corona-App issued by the Austrian Red Cross from March 25, 2020 (SCA DPIA) [6]. However, critical scientific dissections of DPIAs, as this paper intends to do, are not known to the authors.

Before we dive into analyzing the official DPIA, we need to get familiar with the CWA and its technological basis.

1.1 Function and Architecture of the CWA

The main purpose of the CWA is to warn individuals who have had contact with infected persons in the recent past so they can voluntarily self-quarantine. Later on, the functions of storing vaccination and testing certificates were added, but those are ignored here to avoid too much complexity.

The warning functionality is put to practice by the smartphone sending regularly changing strings (pseudonymous temporary identifiers, tempIDs) via Bluetooth at regular intervals using the "Bluetooth Low Energy Beacons" (BTLE) standard, and at the same time receiving the temporary identifiers (tempIDs) from other apps accordingly, when they are in close vicinity [2]. Hence, each app keeps two buckets with the tempIDs of the last fourteen days, one bucket for the tempIDs sent and one for the tempIDs received. Actual location information, for example GPS data, is not processed or even collected by this system. The underlying Bluetooth functionality is managed by the Exposure Notification Framework (ENF or GAEN) provided by Apple and Google in their respective mobile operating systems [7].

In case of positive testing, only the temporary identifiers (the daily seeds, to be precise) sent out by the person during the past 14 days are uploaded to the CWA server. Those uploaded temporary identifiers indicate infectiousness. If any other app has received those tempIDs via Bluetooth, it means that there was a possibly relevant contact event. Therefore the other apps regularly download the current data set of all infection-indicating tempIDs and check for matches, i.e. if they have seen any of those tempIDs. If yes, they calculate locally on the smartphone whether there is a risk of infection based on the duration and proximity of the contact, as well as the state of illness of the infected person at the time of contact. If there is a risk, the user is warned accordingly by the app (not by the server).

Since the server only knows the ever changing tempIDs of infected users, it can neither create a contact history nor calculate the social network of all users [2]. Therefore, this decentralized variant [8] is much more data protection-friendly, yet also more traffic-intensive than a centralized one, e.g. TousAntiCOVID in France or TraceTogether in Singapore. This brings us back to the DPIA.

1.2 Data Protection Impact Assessment (DPIA)

The CWA is part of a European project for large-scale contact tracing under government responsibility. Especially this kind of project needs scrutiny in terms of data protection analysis. To find, analyze and discuss data protection implications the European General Data Protection Regulation (GDPR) provides the instrument of a data protection impact assessment (DPIA), which, in specific cases as this one, is legally mandatory [2]. Art. 35 GDPR ("Data Protection Impact Assessment") states:

(1) *Where a type of processing in particular using new technologies, and taking into account the nature, scope, context and purposes of the processing, is likely to result in a high risk to the rights and freedoms of natural persons, the controller shall, prior to the processing, carry out an assessment of the impact of the envisaged processing operations on the protection of personal data. A single assessment may address a set of similar processing operations that present similar high risks.*
       [...]
(2) *The assessment shall contain at least*

   (a) *a systematic description of the envisaged processing operations and the purposes of the processing, including, where applicable, the legitimate interest pursued by the controller;*
   (b) *an assessment of the necessity and proportionality of the processing operations in relation to the purposes;*
   (c) *an assessment of the risks to the rights and freedoms of data subjects referred to in paragraph 1; and*
   (d) *the measures envisaged to address the risks, including safeguards, security measures and mechanisms to ensure the protection of personal data and to demonstrate compliance with this Regulation taking into account the rights and legitimate interests of data subjects and other persons concerned [9].*

It is essential for a DPIA according to the GDPR, that the focus does not lie on the technology itself, in this case the Corona-Warn-App, but instead the DPIA should focus on the processing procedure as a whole. Such procedure consists of several series of processing activities which can be, in part, supported by technology like an app [2]. All considerations must therefore look beyond the use of "the app" and embrace the whole process including servers, network infrastructure, operating system frameworks and even the parts of the process not using IT like "taking a COVID test". To summarize it, the (boundary of the) app is not the (boundary of the) processing [2].

1.3 Official Handling of Conducting the DPIA

Systems like the CWA can discriminate people and might accustom individuals to be continuously monitored directly in their day-to-day life by a governmental IT system. One way to take up and deal with concerns like that is through public debate based on a high quality data protection impact assessment. By making the official CWA DPIA publicly available, which is not requested by the GDPR, the societal significance of the CWA system was acknowledged and discussing it became possible. In this respect, DPIAs contribute to a systematic public discussion of the surveillance and control aspects of the digitized society.

The initial CWA DPIA had correctly identified some of the existing risks. For example, the problematic role of the Exposure Notification Framework (ENF) of Google and Apple was recognized and analyzed up to the realization "that they jointly developed the ENF according to their ideas and integrated it as a separate system function in their respective operating systems; the storage period of tag keys [...], the configuration parameters [...] and the availability of the ENF are unilaterally determined by Google and Apple. Apps may only access the functions and data of the ENF if unilateral specifications by Apple or Google are met. To that extent, Apple and Google determine the purpose and essential means of processing by the ENF." (Section 8.8.3 in the initial DPIA [3]).

The identification feature "IP address" was also given the essential relevance it deserves, which is often misappropriated elsewhere. From a data protection point of view, it is generally not a matter of obtaining the real name of a person on the basis of IP addresses in order to identify that person. The IP address itself is already the identifying data and therefore personal data, as has also been established in the relevant rulings of the European Court of Justice of 2016 and the German Federal Court of Justice in 2017. In this respect, it is correctly stated in the official DPIA that "insofar and as long as the RKI stores or otherwise processes anonymous data in connection with an IP address on its own, it is therefore personal data for the RKI as a whole." (Section 10.1.1 [3]).

The CWA-DPIA even positively coruscates with its analysis regarding the nature of the data at various points of the processing, when it states, for example: "The list of positive keys of other users downloaded from the [CWA server], which are processed locally on the user's smartphone, are health data for the RKI as long as these data are on the [CWA server], since they indicate a coronavirus infection of the persons behind the respective positive key or the (former) day keys" (Section 10.1.3 [3]). All these points have been aptly worked out, but criticism must nevertheless also be expressed.

As described in detail below, the initial official DPIA has several severe weaknesses, but we want to stress that the official DPIA working group, over time, positively responded to several public contributions as well as to the independent model DPIA mentioned above [5]. The initial shortcomings of the official DPIA might be explained by an initially inexperienced DPIA team with a background only in IT security, but that is speculation on our side [10].

In the following we will focus on the weaknesses found, however, we will not lay out the deep analysis of the initial CWA-DPIA, but only highlight a few, yet essential, exemplary and critical aspects of the CWA-DPIA with regard to methodological, technical and legal deficits.

First, we will list general points of criticism, after which we will address some specific points and finally propose improvements.

2   General Points of Criticism

The initial DPIA report contained many shortcomings, although DPIAs should be part of the standard repertoire of every personal data processing project since May 2016 due to the new obligations of the GDPR. The official CWA had many methodological weaknesses and did not follow a systematic approach to fulfill the requirements of the GDPR. Instead of systematically transforming the normative requirements of data protection law into functional requirements (see the standard data protection model [4]), the initial official DPIA apparently drew the problem definitions from general knowledge on IT security and external attackers. Orientation towards the relevant guidelines of the European Data Protection Board, in particular on consent [11], was also missing. We found three substantial deficiencies which entail many further flaws in the risk analysis of the DPIA. First, the GDPR - and thus a DPIA - never refers to only one selected technical component ("the app"), but always to the processing activity as a whole. Secondly, in the official DPIA there was no consistent data protection-specific attacker model, which systematically focuses on the fundamental rights infringements caused by the data controllers (and the technical operators commissioned by them). And thirdly, the legal constellations and responsibilities regarding risk minimization were not sufficiently presented and assessed.

2.1   Protective Function of a DPIA

The function of a DPIA according to Art. 35 GDPR is to make the risks for fundamental rights of natural persons posed by the data processing visible primarily for the controller itself. We generically adopt "the controller" as a general role designation from the GDPR. This is often provocative because the controller is analytically considered the main attacker for the rights and freedoms of data subjects [2]. Hence, the construction is daring: the controller, who is considered the main aggressor, is at the same time the one who is supposed to determine and then implement measures with which these risks for the data subjects can be reduced to an acceptable level [12]. However, this is at the same time the reason for the standardization of protective provisions by data protection law and for the requirement of a DPIA for particularly risky processing activities. A DPIA report should enable the responsible party to ensure that measures are taken to effectively reduce the identified risks to a acceptable level. However, a DPIA must also explicitly show when significant risks cannot be reduced.

The latter may have the consequence that a processing activity, measured against the requirements of the GDPR, cannot be implemented as planned and is therefore impermissible.

A dismissive discussion of risks completely misses the point of a DPIA, as it becomes particularly clear in the present DPIA report regarding the handling of the operating system functions provided by Google and Apple, and the reference to the fact that the controller is not planning any protective measures here. On the contrary, a DPIA must call for helpful recommendations for protective measures with regard to identified risks, or it must expressively show that the risks remain untreated, i.e. open problems and untreated risks must be named as such. With regard to the problem of the existing blatant dependencies on the manufacturers of smartphone operating systems, it may well be concluded that these uncontrollable proprietary functions should not be used at all due to the lack of sufficient verifiability, and hence untreated vulnerability of the data subjects, of the associated processing on the part of the manufacturers.

2.2 Requirements and Methodology of a DPIA

Article 35 of the GDPR specifies the requirements for a DPIA. The basis is a description of the processing activity, whereby the description necessarily comprises a documentation of the properties of all components used. The methods and guidelines that can be used for this purpose are listed in the FIfF DPIA starting on p. 12 [5]. The main methodological flaw of the official CWA DPIA is, that only the functions of the app are considered, but not the processes of the entire processing with all its data, all IT components used and processes (partially illustrated in the overview of the CWA architecture, Fig. 2, section 8.1 [3]). The integration of the verification hotline into the DPIA points in the right direction, but this could also have been done more consistently (see e.g. Section 10.2.3.5 [3]). The scope of a DPIA is the processing itself (according to Art. 4 (2) GDPR), not just an IT component. In this initial CWA report, although essential components such as the server operation are named in Figures 2 and 16, their functionalities are only roughly outlined. The data flows to the health authorities and the doctors involved would have to be presented in detail, including the legal relationships of all parties involved with each other and ultimately always with reference to the responsible party, the data controller. A proper data protection risk analysis would, for example, have placed great emphasis on the representation of the server(s) to which the tempIDs of Corona infected persons are uploaded. Those servers are precisely the high-risk points that the FIfF DPIA has insistently drawn attention to, because the entire data protection risk depends on the degree of personal reference of the infection-indicating data on the server. According to the initial DPIA, it remains arcane and non-transparent which data protection-relevant characteristics the servers involved have, which transactions and data are logged, evaluated or deleted later. A vague statement that "on the part of the RKI, it is planned to delete the IP address from the server log files on the CWA server and CDN-Magenta immediately after responding to a request" and therefore "the personal reference described above in connection with an IP address would only exist for the RKI for a 'technical second'" (Section 10.1.1 [3]) is far from sufficient, because this moment in the entire processing chain is the most sensitive spot, since the tempIDs of infected persons are personalized here via IP address. Even a sincere promise made by the responsible party is not a protective measure, it's just resorting to trusting the powerful actor. This is the opposite of data protection. Those aspects have been greatly improved in later versions of the official DPIA, even with citations to the FIfF DPIA.

Moreover, a DPIA as such should not be considered or created as a "living document" (Section 1 [3]). A DPIA report must claim a certain closure of the analysis plus findings and conclude with concrete recommendations for risk mitigation. Nevertheless, the controller of the processing activity must of course be able to react to further changes in the context of the processing activity. This, however, is the function of a data protection management. This means that a finished DPIA has to be handed over to a data protection management, in this case to the hopefully actually existing data protection management system, who then acts on the insights produced. Appointing a data protection officer at the RKI is not a proper data protection management system.

2.3 The Processing Activity

For a meaningful description of the processing activity as a systemic context, it is recommended to a) describe the sequence of purpose, purpose description, purpose separation and purpose limitation, as proposed by the SDM V2 [4], and b) to orientate oneself at least using the 14 sub processes that are listed as components of a processing in Art. 4 (2) of the GDPR. The presentation of the functional properties essential under data protection law can then be created along the risks formed from the principles of Article 5 GDPR, or in the case of a primarily functional orientation, from the compact assurance objectives of the SDM. In concrete terms, orienting oneself not to the procedure, but mainly to the CWA app, has then led to the fatal assumption in Section 10.1 [3], namely that the data processed locally or "offline" on the smartphone are not considered part of the controller's processing activity.

The CWA app is, of course, part of the process insofar as it contributes to the achievement of the purpose. It is also a product of technical design by or on behalf of the controller and thus determines in principle the possible consequences of the use of technology. Last but not least, the responsible party controls and manages the patching and update management process of the CWA app (via the provision of new signed software versions in the "App or Play Store"), in which the CWA users participate, and thus also influences the procedure and its consequences in the future. This would have been evident in a procedure-oriented analysis as opposed to an application-oriented analysis. The consequences to be considered downstream here would then not only have to deal with the risk of de-anonymisation by the controller itself (Section 10.1.2 [3]), but also with risks due to software errors or operating system functions used, which could, for example, lead to de-anonymisation by third parties. To ensure that this does not happen, a level of protection appropriate to the risk must also be guaranteed on the smartphones (Art. 32(1) GDPR), offline or not.

Although the DPIA understands "Corona-Warn-App" to mean not only the app itself, but also the CWA servers in many places, there is no clear mention of the servers. However, this area in particular is sensitive and relevant for the (non-existent) attacker model. Because apart from attacks by third parties, it is the server operators themselves who can relatively easily influence the processing on the server. For example, it would have been necessary to explain how the CWA server differs from the other servers (test result server, portal server, verification server, CDN) with respect to the risks posed by their function.

Furthermore, there is no systematic description of interfaces or communication relationships as well as their purpose, type of information transferred, types of access and associated protection measures. This must then show, above all, the extent to which data is forwarded to other (joint) controllers or for commissioned data processing, e.g. from or to doctors' practices, laboratories, SAP/Telekom data centers or operating system manufacturers, in order to identify risky points for potential misappropriation (in accordance with the protection goal of non-linkability and confidentiality). They are of "crucial importance for the legal accountability, controllability and auditability of data flows" (SDM V2 [4], p. 39). Those aspects have been greatly improved in later versions of the official DPIA, even with citations to the FIfF DPIA.

2.4 Risk Modeling

Another conceptual methodological flaw is the lack of data protection-specific risk modeling [12]. This is obviously due to the general lack of sufficient orientation in operational data protection. From a data protection perspective, the controller itself is considered the main aggressor on the rights and freedoms of natural persons; the principles from Article 5 GDPR then form the criteria with which risks are to be observed and assessed. This methodical approach has been considered good DPIA practice ("state of the art") since 2017 at the latest among those who know how to distinguish operational data protection from IT security issues.

The specific data protection risk for CWA users is that the infringement on fundamental rights by the controller and "his" data processing is too intensive and the data protection principles are not fulfilled. In concrete terms, this means that, for example, the confidentiality, integrity and purpose limitation of data processing are not adequately secured at any point in the entire processing chain (and not just on the smartphone itself) and that there are no audit and test options (transparency) for identifying whether the protective measures are actually effective and demonstrably function securely.

All this aims towards the protection of those affected by processing [13], oftentimes from the processor itself, which does not correspond to the goal of IT security which protects the organisation and the organization's systems.

Therefore, such necessary assurances as in the glossary (section 4.1 [3]) are too vague and useless when it states, for example, that "the contact record can also be actively deleted as a whole by the CWA user at any time. The data in the operating system (collected and own day keys) are not deleted, but remain stored for 2 weeks in the protected operating system memory." At this point, the ability to control by the CWA users is removed and another transparency problem is added. It remains unclear what happens to the contact records in the following. For example, can this information be uploaded to the server despite being deleted? What role does it play that the operating system storage is a specially protected area? Does the fact that it is a specially protected area have any impact at all on the risks to fundamental rights or on their minimization if this area is not controllable by any of the concerned entities such as the RKI, CWA users, DP supervisory authorities?

The preparation of a DPIA is, within the GDPR, again an essential requirement to implement Art. 25 GDPR. Art. 25 requires that data protection requirements are already to be taken into account in the planning phase, i.e. in particular the insights, assessments and ultimately the recommendations from the DPIA. A GDPR-compliant DPIA report can therefore never be available two days, or as in this case, ten hours before the delivery of an application and the start of the actual processing for a specific purpose. Such a report cannot then serve prudent planning but only the formal legalization of the procedure. This time delay is also critical with regard to the inclusion of the point of view of the data subjects (Art. 35(9) GDPR), since the nature, scope and circumstances of this processing suggest a social debate in advance. Only an early publication creates publicity and thus the conditions for the inclusion of different points of view for exactly this processing activity. Passively waiting for specialist publications and media reports does not do justice to this responsibility. From the project management's point of view, postponing the go-live would therefore have been the right approach.

3   Concrete Constructive Criticism

In addition to the more general comments above, some selected detailed and exemplary issues are now outlined, at times even with constructive remarks to solve the issues at hand.

3.1   Separation of the Personal Reference When Uploading the Positive Keys

As briefly mentioned above, a very sensitive, if not the central, point for affected individuals exists at the moment when the tempIDs of those who tested positive are uploaded to the CWA server and thereby become positive keys. Through the metadata of the connection, specifically the IP address at the time of upload, the infected person is directly identifiable. Trusting in simple deletion of the corresponding entries in the log files by the operator is not sufficient in the case of such a guaranteed high risk for the affected persons (Section 10.1.1 [3]). Looking back at the long history of anti-terror and security laws restricting fundamental rights this can change quickly. This risk pertains, even when the server operator is legally or practically not able to put a name on the IP address, in data protection the IP address is the name, metaphorically.

Hence, not only technical safeguards must be imposed in order to make de-pseudonymisation or other identification of app users sufficiently difficult. This must be specifically prevented by legal, organisational and technical measures, as is explained in the recommendations in the FIfF-DPIA (see DPIA Chapter 9 – Recommendations [5]). In organisational terms, the controller must establish a strategically mixed structure, including operational measures in order to achieve this goal. The responsible party - i.e., the RKI - can, for example, strategically select several different operators: one operates the input nodes into the network and the other one operates the servers on which the data is stored. Operationally, the separation of personal data within organizations should be ensured by an appropriate departmental structure, separation of functions and separation of roles, etc., which enforce the informational separation of powers (i.e. functional differentiation) within the organization. By far the most effective protection consists of a technical bundle of measures to ensure sufficient sender anonymity at the interface to the infrastructure of the operators.

After all, only those organizations that have no interest of their own in the data can be considered as operators to create a "trusted infrastructure". This would also provide effective protection against the obligation to hand over data, even to security authorities who simply give it a try. The omission of such a critical component of the data protection architecture could be judged as a serious ground for stopping the processing at all. One should not rely on fictions such as "user confidence that the operator will behave in a legally compliant manner and will only release data to law enforcement authorities if the legal requirement is met" (Design Decision D-11–1 [3]) when it comes to identifying risks. For legal protection, the separation of the personal reference can be stipulated by an accompanying law strictly limiting the use of the data. This aspect is still an ongoing debate.

3.2 Dealing with Risks at the ENF

The recourse to techniques and services of the operating systems Google Android and Apple iOS is another very central point of data protection scrutiny at which it becomes architecturally particularly tricky. The associated risks are only indirectly addressed in the initial DPIA and only by rejecting responsibility for them. The retreat to "not knowing" but "trusting" at the very beginning of the DPIA report (ENF, p. 2 [3]) is inappropriate and does not meet the requirements of relentlessly explaining risks in detail and living up to the controller's responsibility, since the GDPR requires exactly taking responsibility for the functioning and data protection compliance of the entire system. Especially when it is agreed on p. 43 that "the CWA App and the ENF [...] are central components of the overall CWA system" [3]. At this point, not only methodological weaknesses, but also legal and political ones arise. These risks must be recognized, dealt with and at least put under legal conditions by the actors in charge. Unlike in the context of IT security, where an organisation can chose to accept the risks, these risks can not simply be taken, since they affect the data subject directly [14]. At this point, a proper DPIA would have to examine the concept of "joint responsibility" and recommend ways of structuring the CWA in a legally compliant manner with obligations for the OS manufacturers. It is undoubtedly a delicate matter to impose the legal and practical consequences of this onto Google and Apple, especially if one is dependent on their technologies. But to completely forego the political and legal discussion and abort an exploration of the possibilities right from the start is not a solution and negates the democratic foundation that the people (in the form of the government) make the rules.

Of course, the results of an analysis can be very unpleasant, but the consequences for those affected are all the more so. So if "own findings about the inner workings [...] cannot be obtained because this framework is implemented for security reasons in a way that precludes an investigation", then it is not possible to simply "rely on the correctness of the processing in the frameworks and the descriptions" (Section 1 [3]). It is exactly the task of a serious DPIA to ring the alarm at this point, not play down the risks! An inspection of the source code of the ENF would be the least that would even come close to a protective measure and until then, the risks have to be simply labeled as unmitigated.

Another avoidance behaviour we found in the Initial DPIA is the protective claim that "by using an Android or iOS smartphone, users [have] expressed that they fundamentally trust these manufacturers or, in any case, have come to terms with the privacy risks associated with using a smartphone from these manufacturers for personal purposes or have otherwise adapted their usage behavior accordingly" (Section 11.2.4 [3]). However, unlike universal and basic multi-purpose operating system functions such as Wi-Fi, cellular, camera or data storage, the ENF is a highly specialized service created solely for and functioning only with official contact tracing apps, and thus necessary for CWA operation. It is therefore not a normal "infrastructure component" of the smartphone operating system, but an integral part (i.e. means) of the app and its purpose. With regard to the problem of the existing blatant dependencies on the manufacturers of smartphone operating systems, it may well be concluded that these uncontrollable proprietary functions are too risky and should not be used at all due to the lack of sufficient verifiability of the associated processing on the part of the manufacturers. However not using them and still providing a CWA is only an option in the Google Android ecosystem, if at all, as demonstrated with the open source replacement framework called microG. This aspect is still an ongoing debate.

3.3 Consent and Responsibility

Pursuant to Article 35(1) of the GDPR, the DPA must be carried out by the data controller. The data protection responsibility for a processing activity cannot simply be assigned to an authority or claimed "The RKI [is] the controller within the meaning of Article 4 No. 7 of the GDPR for the processing of users' personal data associated with the operation of the CWA" (Sections 6.1 and 8.8.1 [3]). A data protection responsibility is to be determined in accordance with the regulation in Art. 4 No. 7 GDPR. According to this, whoever determines the purposes and means of the processing is responsible. Something else can only apply if the purposes and means of this processing are specified by a law. Only in this case can the controller be determined or can the criteria specified in a law provide for the designation of the controller in accordance with legal requirements. Such a legal determination of responsibility has not been made so far. For all processing operations of the CWA, it would therefore have been necessary to determine specifically which body or bodies determine the purposes of the processing and who determines the means for this purpose. According to the project outline (Sections 5 and 8.8.4.1 [3]), the Federal Ministry of Health has determined the purposes of the processing (warning of infection and notification of infection) and the means, namely the use of an app. In the DPIA, it would have been necessary to discuss which tasks with regard to the determination of the means and purposes actually pass to the RKI in the context of the operation.

In the same way, it would have been necessary to determine whether a joint responsibility with Apple and Google arises through the integration of the ENF functionality and what consequences result from this (Section 8.8.3 [3]). For according to the CWA DPIA, neither the Federal Ministry nor the RKI nor their processors have any influence on this part of the app functionality. However, it cannot be denied that a joint purpose-driven determination of the ENF has taken place, as the Federal Ministry has publicly opted for the technology offered by Apple and Google [5]. The responsibility does not require that the technical details are also determined in high resolution by the controller. However, insofar as joint responsibility is assumed, reference should have been made to Art. 26 GDPR and the resulting risks. The discussion of the responsibility of the app users and thus a reversal of the role as data subjects testifies to a weakness in understanding of data protection law. At most, it could be considered with regard to the storage and comparison of the positive keys of other users.

In view of the fact that the CWA-DPIA assumes the legal basis of consent, the essential subject matter of which is precisely this processing, these statements are just as disconcerting as those that address the rejection of responsibility for the data subject data. This is because the exercise of data subjects' rights (e.g. revocation) vis-à-vis the controller cannot lead to the data subjects being held responsible (Section 8.8.3 [3]). In demarcation to the responsibility, the processors would rather have had to be determined and the risks arising from commissioned processing would have had to be discussed. In Section 10 [3], a structure more oriented towards the legal requirements would have been helpful.

The basic prerequisite for an evaluation under data protection law is an understanding of Article 1 (2) of the GDPR with regard to the rights and freedoms of natural persons, the basic principles of data protection law and the terminology. When determining and dealing with the reference to persons as such, the question of the scope (as posed in Section 10.1 [3]) of the personal data is irrelevant. This only plays a role in assessing the risk posed by processing large amounts of personal data. The non-resolution of the personal link between content and transport data in the server log files (Section 10.1.1 [3]) is a risk that should also have been identified as such and at least placed under legal conditions. This is one of the main risks of possible attack scenarios (see above) and would have to be the subject of regular audits from now on.

The differentiation of the data categories according to their processing location (personal data "at the RKI" in Section 10.1.1 [3] and local data processing on the smartphone in Section 10.1.2 [3]) makes sense in principle, but the DPIA is not the appropriate place to discuss questions of responsibility based on the data categories.

Moreover, as mentioned above, local processing (Secton 10.1.2 [3]) on the apps is not outside the de facto sphere of influence of the controller, who determines the design of the technology and thus the ways in which users can, for example, express their consents through explicit actions. The users also have no influence on the technical design of the CWA. Why local data processing should involve categories of personal data at all remains unclear and should have been addressed in the description of the processing. It can be assumed that this section was actually intended to discuss the categories of personal data processed on the smartphones, apparently with the aim of subsuming the controller out of the procedure. The reference to the concerns of the German Federal Commissioner for Data Protection and Freedom of Information about denying responsibility for processing on smartphones points in this direction.

These discussions fail to recognize that the reference to a person does not depend on whether this can be established by the controller at all or at any time. Rather, the requirements of data protection by design (Article 25 GDPR) require that the data protection principles be implemented effectively. Measures do not change the responsibility for the CWA procedure. Contrary to what is stated in the CWA DPIA, according to the

Breyer ruling of the ECJ (C-582/14), it is important that the person responsible "has legal means which allow him to identify the person concerned on the basis of the additional information available to that person's Internet access provider" (para. 49). The RKI as operator also has such legal means to access IP addresses of users. It is thus in principle able to trace the identifiers of the daily or positive keys back to the users. The fact that the data controller cannot attribute the data at Google and Apple does not change their personal reference, but once again underlines the joint responsibility for their processing in the procedure [15].

Art. 5 para. 2 in conjunction with. (1)(a) of the GDPR require the controller to prove the lawfulness of the processing. Section 10.2 of the initial CWA DPIA [3] deals with this question. It should be noted here that the fulfillment of the requirements of a legal basis is a necessary condition for the lawfulness of the processing. However, the legal basis alone does not make processing lawful. It must be supplemented by the fulfillment of further requirements that the GDPR places on data controllers.

With regard to consent as a legal basis, it should be noted that its effectiveness cannot be assumed as a general rule, but that the existence of the requirements must be proven in each individual case, i.e. for each consenting person and for each purpose. The requirements for consent are derived from Art. 6 (1) sentence 1 lit. a, 7 and 4 No. 11 GDPR. The EDSA has issued an opinion on the interpretation and application (Guidelines 05/2020 on consent under Regulation 2016/679). At this point, it should be noted that pursuant to Article 70 (1) of the GDPR, it is the task of the EDSA to provide guidance on the interpretation of the GDPR; reading and observing this guidance in the context of the DPIA on the CWA is strongly recommended. Art. 4 No. 11 requires that consent is given 1) voluntarily, 2) specifically, 3) informed and 4) with an unambiguous expression of will in the form of a statement or unambiguous affirmative act.

A distinction must be made between consent as a legal basis with regard to the procedure and consent to the processing of special categories of data pursuant to Art. 9 (2) lit a GDPR. The DPIA also lacks the necessary level of detail of the presentation and risk discussion here. Particularly in the case of a processing of health data using a tracing technology that is new for these purposes, a detailed discussion would have been necessary.

A DPIA is also not just about repeating legally prescribed criteria, but requires a discussion of the requirements with regard to ensuring their fulfilment, i.e. with an operationalization of normative requirements into functional requirements. For example, it would have been necessary to elaborate on what information about the procedure and its purposes is required for informed consent, what risks may arise, and references to how this has been implemented in the CWA or how the risks are addressed.

A reference to the fact that "it is not evident that this information could not be reliably conveyed to the user in advance of granting consent" (Section 10.2.3.2 [3]) is by no means sufficient for this. It is not possible to conclude from an action of the user that he or she is informed. Reference should also be made to the EDSA document regarding voluntariness. In particular, the CWADPIA lacks a discussion of the fact that use of the app when receiving a warning is associated with a symptomindependent testing option; this option is not afforded to non-users of the CWA. The indication that the legislator is not currently planning to make use of the app compulsory or to make it a prerequisite for relaxation is only partially suitable for a risk assessment, also because members of the Bundestag and the Landtag have already publicly made precisely this demand. Here, for example, the possibility of a "second wave" would have had to be discussed and requirements formulated for those responsible or the legislator as to how voluntariness can be permanently ensured.

Neither the fact that not all citizens have an app-enabled smartphone nor the fact that people could install an app on an old or second smartphone in order to prove the conditions of voluntary use are suitable arguments. Current and former discussions [16] about the CWA as an admission requirement or other benefits associated with it demonstrate the everyday relevance of this risk [17]. Crucially, however, the requirements of consent must be present in each individual user, and so must voluntariness.

A DPIA must address the question of how to assess a situation in which a majority or at least a large number of users can no longer be assumed to use the data voluntarily due to feelings of solidarity or employer coercion. At the very least, a legal regulation would have been a measure to be addressed. On this subject of the penetration of the population with CWA-capable devices and their voluntary use, two opposing statements can be found. Thus, with regard to voluntariness, it is stated: "In this respect, too, the voluntariness of the use of CWA could turn into a de facto compulsion through social pressure. However, it should be borne in mind that a significant proportion of the population do not own a smartphone at all, or do not own a suitable smartphone, especially if they are particularly young, old or have a low purchasing power." (Section 10.2.3.3 [3]) In the section on suitability, there is again a contrary expectation: "It is assumed that a large proportion of the population owns and mostly carries a suitable smartphone and that BLE technology may in principle be suitable for carrying out sufficiently precise distance measurement for logging contacts in the context of risk identification." (Section 11.2.2 [3]) So what is the basic assumption? Either the assumption on voluntariness or the assumption on suitability must be dropped by the responsible party. This aspect is still an ongoing debate.

3.4 Open Questions

Some of the aspects outlined here have been taken up by the official DPIA team and included into the current DPIA [3], because we pointed them towards them, but many other key data protection questions remain open that would have to be addressed and analyzed in a proper DPIA. How does the generation of TeleTANs for health offices and hotline work? What happens on the portal server? How does the registration token behave, does it exclude traceability via QR code? What settings can the CWA user make? Who is the actual person responsible, who is the commissioning party, who has which responsibilities based on instructions? Can the RKI simply become the controller without legal assignment? Yet, questions of properly describing processing procedures, elaborating of sub components and fleshing out the data protection specific attacker models are brilliantly done in the current version of the DPIA.

4 Conclusion

Data protection cannot be implemented exclusively by technology and therefore cannot be evaluated by pure technology analysis of the IT components as well. The existing risks that arise from the activities of the responsible parties and the contracted service providers must be identified along the entire chain of processing steps and protective measures to reduce them must be proposed, discussed and evaluated. In order to identify a benchmark for the quality: A DPIA report should itself comply with the principles of Article 5 GDPR and the data protection goals. The legal dispute must specify the requirements to which the legal, technical and organisational measures for risk minimisation are subsequently aligned. Such a discussion was missing for the critical points of responsibility, purpose limitation of processing, the existence of the use of consent as well as the voluntariness of the use and the proof of voluntariness. The initially evaded risk discussion lead to the fact that an essential measure for risk reduction for the data subjects, namely the enactment of a law that binds the controller and other interested parties to the app, was not even discussed. It is not the purpose of a DPIA to justify the processing of personal data in the context of a technical solution, as was done in particular in the assessment of the proportionality of the processing in the initial DPIA. Rather, it is the task of the DPIA to identify the risks arising from the processing, the safeguards taken to that end and, in particular, to focus on unaddressed risks. The present official DPIA made a big step in this right direction [3].

References

1. RKI – Robert Koch-Institut: Corona-Warn-App: Documentation (2021). https://github.com/corona-warn-app/cwa-documentation . Accessed 2 Feb 2022
2. Rehak, R., Kühne, C.R.: The processing goes far beyond "the app" – privacy issues of decentralized digital contact tracing using the example of the German Corona-Warn-App. In: Proceedings of 2022 IEEE 6th International Conference on Cryptography, Security and Privacy (CSP 2022) (forthcoming)
3. RKI – Robert Koch-Institut: (Archived) Version 1.0 of the official DPIA of the Corona-Warn-App (2020). https://web.archive.org/web/20200616232321/https://www.coronawarn.app/assets/documents/cwa-datenschutz-folgenabschaetzung.pdf. The current version can be found here https://www.coronawarn.app/assets/documents/cwa-datenschutz-folgenabschaetzung.pdf. Accessed 2 Feb 2022
4. SDM - UAG "Standard Data Protection Model" of the AK Technik of the Independent Data Protection Supervisory Authorities of the Federation and the Länder: The Standard Data Protection Model – A method for Data Protection advising and controlling on the basis of uniform protection goals, AK Technik of the Independent Data Protection Supervisory Authorities of the Federation and the Länder (2020). https://www.datenschutzzentrum.de/uploads/sdm/SDM-Methodology_V2.0b.pdf. Accessed 2 Feb 2022
5. Bock, K., Kühne, C.R., Mühlhoff, R., et al.: Data protection impact assessment for the corona app, 29 April 29 2020. SSRN: https://ssrn.com/abstract=3588172. Accessed 2 Feb 2022
6. Tschohl, C., Scheichenbauer, H., Kastelitz, M., et al.: Bericht über die Datenschutz-Folgenabschätzung für die Anwendung Stopp Corona-App des Österreichischen Roten Kreuzes (OeRK), Version 2.0. vom 04.08.2020. https://www.roteskreuz.at/fileadmin/user_upload/PDF/Datenschutz/Datenschutz-Folgenabschaetzung-Bericht_OeRK_StopCoronaApp_04-08-2020_V2.0_final.pdf. Accessed 2 Feb 2022

7. Google/Apple: Exposure Notification Framework – ENF / Googe-Apple-Exposure-Notification – GAEN (2020). https://developer.apple.com/documentation/exposurenotific ation and https://www.google.com/covid19/exposurenotifications/. Accessed 2 Feb 2022
8. DP3T – Decentralized Privacy-Preserving Proximity Tracing (2020) EPFL and ETH Zurich advance digital contact tracing project. https://actu.epfl.ch/news/epfl-and-eth-zurichadvance-digital-contact-tracin/ (last visited 2/2/2022)
9. GDPR – General Data Protection Regulation. Regulation (EU) 2016/679. https://eurlex.eur opa.eu/eli/reg/2016/679/oj. Accessed 2 Feb 2022
10. Pohle, J.: Datenschutz und Technikgestaltung: Geschichte und Theorie des Datenschutzes aus informatischer Sicht und Folgerungen für die Technikgestaltung. Dissertation, Mathematisch-Naturwissenschaftliche Fakultät, Humboldt-Universität zu Berlin (2018). https://edoc.hu-ber lin.de/handle/18452/19886. Accessed 2 Feb 2022
11. Guidelines 05/2020 on consent under Regulation 2016/679. https://edpb.europa.eu/sites/edpb/ files/files/file1/edpb_guidelines_202005_consent_en.pdf. Accessed 2 Feb 2022
12. Rost, M.: Risks in the context of data protection/Risiken im Datenschutz. In: vorgänge – Zeitschrift für Bürgerrechte und Gesellschaftspolitik **57**(1/2), 79–92 (2018). English version. https://www.maroki.de/pub/privacy/Rost_Martin_2019-02_Risk:_8types_v1.pdf. Accessed 2 Feb 2022
13. Rost, M.: Zur Soziologie des Datenschutzes. Datenschutz und Datensicherheit - DuD **37**(2), 85–91 (2013). https://doi.org/10.1007/s11623-013-0023-3
14. Steinmüller, W.: Grundfragen des Datenschutzes, Gutachten, BT-Drucksache 6/3826, German Bundestag (1972)
15. Article 29 Data Protection Working Party. Opinion 4/2007 on the concept of personal data. Working Paper 136 (2007). https://ec.europa.eu/justice/article29/documentation/opinion-rec ommendation/files/2007/wp136_en.pdf. Accessed 2 Feb 2022
16. Felschen, C.: Geplante Corona-App soll Daten doch dezentral speichern (2020). https:// www.zeit.de/digital/datenschutz/2020-04/datenschutz-corona-tracing-app-dezentrale-speich erung. Accessed 2 Feb 2022
17. Greis, F.: Steuervorteile für Corona-App-Nutzer gefordert (2020). https://www.golem.de/ news/lockerungsdebattesteuervorteile-fuer-corona-app-nutzer-gefordert-2004148137.html. Accessed 2 Feb 2022

Author Index

Printed in the United States
by Baker & Taylor Publisher Services.

Printed in the United States
by Baker & Taylor Publisher Services